# The Art of Poetry vo

C000180646

Eduqas poetry anthology

With thanks to Matthew Curry, Johanna Harrison and Neil Jones. And to my family for letting me hide away and keep writing.

Published by Peripeteia Press Ltd.

First published April 2017

ISBN: 978-0-9954671-6-3

Peripeteia.webs.com

# Contents

# General Introduction to the The Art of Poetry series

The philosopher Nietzsche described his work as 'the greatest gift that [mankind] has ever been given'. The Elizabethan poet Edmund Spenser hoped his epic, **The Faerie Queene,** would magically transform its readers into noblemen. In comparison, our aims for *The Art of Poetry* series of books are a little more modest. Fundamentally we aim to provide books that will be of maximum use to English students and their teachers. In our experience, few students read essays on poems, yet, whatever specification they are studying, they have to write analytical essays on poetry. So, we've offering some models, written in a lively, accessible and, we hope, engaging style. We believe that the essay as a form needs demonstrating and championing, especially as so many revision books for students present information in broken down note form.

For Volume 1 we chose canonical poems for several reasons: Firstly, they are simply great poems, well worth reading and studying; secondly, we chose poems from across time so that they sketch in outline major developments in English poetry, from the Elizabethan period up until the present day, so that the volume works as an introduction to poetry and poetry criticism. Our popular volumes 2-5 focused on poems set at A-level by the Edexcel and AQA boards respectively. Volumes 6 and 7 tackled AQA's GCSE anthology and volume 9 Edexcel's anthology. In this current volume, we turn our focus again to GCSE, providing critical support for students reading poems from Eduqas's poetry anthology. In particular, we hope our book will inspire those students aiming to reach the very highest grades.

# Introduction to Volume 10

Eduqas have arranged their rich array of poems in alphabetical order and an obvious strategy for highlighting their inter-relationships is to rearrange the poems chronologically. Doing so, we find there are six distinct chronological groupings. As the 'post-1789' tag indicates, the first group of poems was written by the first wave of Romantic poets in the tumultuous wake of the French Revolution. Blake's nightmarish vision of **London** and Wordsworth's retreat into the tranquillity of childhood are both shadowed by this huge historical event. [Wordsworth completed the first version of **The Prelude** in the late 1790s and it includes a section about his time in France]. The same could be said for a second, almost a sub-group, formed by the second generation Romantic poets whose work features in the anthology. Certainly, Shelley's **Ozymandias,** with its depiction of a hubristic tyrant, can be seen as a product of a turbulent time and expresses a typically Romantic veneration for the power of nature. Keats's celebration of autumn and Byron's infatuation with beauty are more obliquely related to this socio-historical context, perhaps in terms of seeking sanctuaries away from the continuing turmoil on the world stage. As we shall see, some critics, however, have read Keats's Ode through a political lense. The Romantics' veneration of nature connects their poems to many others in the anthology. Hughes' **Hawk Roosting**, for example, would make a striking comparison.

From the Romantics we jump forward a little in time to a small, third group of poems from the Victorian period; Barrett-Browning's **Sonnet 43**, Hardy's **A Wife in London** and from across the pond, Dickinson's **As Imperceptibly as Grief**. More emotionally restrained than their Romantic precursors, these poems develop key overarching themes of the collection, such as love and relationships and the experience of conflict. Superficially at least, Dickinson's poem also continues the theme of human interaction with nature. Obviously conflict is the major subject of Wilfred Owen's **Dulce et Decorum Est,** in which the poet expresses his pity for the suffering of soldiers in warfare, as Hardy had done before him for a wife widowed by the Boer War. Compassion is, of course, another form of love. As a poem from the first two decades of the twentieth century, Dulce et Decorum Est is in its own group.

WWI is the context and subject of Owen's poem; the aftermath of WWII, socially, psychologically, aesthetically, is the backdrop to the fifth group of poems, ones by Heaney, Hughes and Larkin. The Irish poet Seamus Heaney's **Death of a Naturalist** explores another source of conflict, this time between man and nature, connecting it to the Romantic poems of Keats, Shelley, and through its focus on childhood and growing up with Wordsworth in particular. Heaney's theme of innocence giving way to experience also links him to Blake. Of course, as we've intimated, Hughes' take on nature is startlingly different from conventional poetic depictions. His utterly unsentimental, ruthleslly red-in-tooth-and-claw version would make for an interesting comparison with Keats's appreciation of the generous abundance of nature. Famously Larkin and Hughes did not get along and, despite being written in a similar period, their poems could hardly be more different in subject, tone and style. While Hughes sought to capture the true timeless essence of nature, Larkin's ironic, urbane voice ponders the ills of modern society. This focus on urban living connects **Afternoons** to Blake's **London** and to Dharker's poem **Living Space**.

The sixth and last group is of modern poems, written in recent decades. This group includes poems from the States, such as Rita Dove's, as well as a poem from Wales by Owen Sheers and a multicultural poem by the Scottish Pakistani Imtiaz Dharker. Armitage's **The Manhunt** and Duffy's **Valentine** complete this final group. Once again, some common themes can be traced back and across the anthology as a whole. Dove's poem provides a snapshot of a loving relationship and, as such, could be compared to Byron's, Barrett-Browning's, Dickinson's as well as to Duffy's and Armitage's poems. Sometimes there will be more similarities, as with **Sonnet 43**, whereas with other comparisons there will be more differences, as with Valentine. **Mametz Wood** takes us back to WWI, only this time approached from a modern perspective looking back into history. Though triggered by modern wars, Armitage's poem shifts our attention to the continuing psychological impact of armed conflict on a couple long after the fighting has stopped. The focus on the husband/wife relationship links his poem back to Hardy's exploration of the impact of the Boer War.

Another way of grouping these poems would be around themes. Although, no doubt you'll be able to find more, there seem to be around five distinct groupings, with some poems appearing in more than one group:

Group 1: Humans & Nature: Excerpt from The Prelude, Ozymandias, To Autumn, As Imperceptibly as Grief; Death of a Naturalist and Hawk Roosting

Group 2: War & conflict: A Wife in London, The Soldier, Dulce et Decorum Est, The Manhunt, Mametz Wood

Group 3: Love & relationships: She Walks in Beauty, Sonnet 43, As Imperceptibly as Grief, A Wife in London, Valentine, Cozy Apologia

Group 4: The use and abuse of power: London, Ozymandias, She Walks in Beauty, Dulce et Decorum Est, Hawk Roosting, Valentine

Group 5: The individual and urban life: London, Afternoons, Living Space.

## The Exams

Poetry features on both components of the Eduqas GCSE English Literature course. In Component 1 pupils have to answer two questions on poems from the anthology. Worth 15 marks, question one will ask for an analysis of one named poem which will be printed on the question paper. Worth 25 marks, question two will ask pupils to compare the presentation of the major topic of this poem with its treatment in one other poem of their choice from the anthology. The key things to remember are that these questions test:

- Your ability to analyse the poems closely, focusing on how writers use language devices to explore ideas
- Your alertness to differences and similarities in treatment of this topic between poems
- The awareness you demonstrate of the influence of contexts on the poems. By contexts, Eduqas mean, 'period, location, social structure and literary contexts, such as genres'.

On Component 2 pupils will face two questions following a similar pattern to those on Component 1. Question one requires close reading of an unseen poem; question two asks pupils to compare this poem's treatment of its major concern to the way it is presented in another unseen poem. Again the questions are marked out of 15 and 25.

To succeed on both components you need to:

- Develop an excellent appreciation of the anthology poems
- Prepare for a range of possible comparisons between them
- Ensure you know and can apply key contexts
- Develop your critical essay writing style
- Develop an approach or methodology for tackling unseen poems.

We'll address those last points in the next section.

# How to analyse a poem [seen or unseen]

### A list of ingredients, not a recipe

Firstly, what not to do: sometimes pupils have been so programmed to spot poetic features such as alliteration that they start analysis of a poem with close reading of these micro aspects of technique. This is never a good idea. A far better strategy is to begin by trying to develop an overall understanding of what you think the poem is about. While, obviously, all these poems are about relationships of some sort or other, the nature of these relationships vary widely what they have say about this topic is also highly varied. Once you've established the central concerns, you can delve into the poem's interior, examining its inner workings in the light of these. And you should be flexible enough to adapt, refine or even reject your initial thoughts in the light of your investigation. The essential thing is to make sure that whether you're discussing imagery or stanza form, sonic effects or syntax, enjambment or vocabulary, you always explore the significance of the feature in terms of meanings and effect.

Someone once compared texts to cakes. When you're presented with a cake the first thing you notice is what it looks like. Probably the next thing you'll do is taste it and find out if you like the flavour. This aesthetic experience will come first. Only later might you investigate the ingredients and how it was made. Adopting a uniform reading strategy is like a recipe; it sets out what you must, do step by step, in a predetermined order. This can be helpful, especially when you start reading and analysing poems. Hence in our first volume in The Art of Poetry series we explored each poem under the same subheadings of narrator, characters, imagery, patterns of sound, form & structure and contexts, and all our essays followed essentially the same direction. Of course, this is a reasonable strategy for reading poetry and will stand you in good stead. However, this present volume takes a different, more flexible approach, because this book is designed for students aiming for levels 7 to 9, or A to A* in old currency, and to reach the highest levels your work needs to be a bit more conceptual, critical and individual. Writing frames are useful for beginners, like stabilisers when you learn to ride a bike. But, if you wish to write top level essays you need to develop your own frames.

Read our essays and you'll find that they all include the same principle ingredients – detailed, 'fine-grained' reading of crucial elements of poetry, imagery, form, rhyme and so forth - but each essay starts in a different way and each one has a slightly different focus or weight of attention on the various aspects that make up a poem. Once you feel you have mastered the apprentice strategy of reading all poems in the same way, we strongly recommend you put this generic essay recipe approach to one side and move on to a new way of reading, an approach that can change depending on the nature of the poem you're reading.

**Follow your nose**

Having established what you think a poem is about - its theme and what is interesting about the poet's treatment of the theme [the conceptual bit] - rather than then working through a pre-set agenda, decide what you honestly think are the most interesting aspects of the poem and start analysing these closely. This way your response will be original [a key marker of a top band essay] and you'll be writing about material you find most interesting. In other words, you're foregrounding yourself as an individual, critical reader. These most interesting aspects might be ideas or technique based, or both.

Follow your own, informed instincts, trust in your own critical intelligence as a reader. If you're writing about material that genuinely interests you, your writing is likely to be interesting for the examiner too. And, obviously, take advice to from your teacher too, use their expertise.

Because of the focus on sonic effects and imagery other aspects of poems are often overlooked by students. It is a rare student, for instance, who notices how punctuation works in a poem and who can write about it convincingly. Few students write about the contribution of the unshowy function words, such as pronouns, prepositions or conjunctions, yet these words are crucial to any text. Of course, it would be a highly risky strategy to focus your whole essay on a seemingly innocuous and incidental detail of a poem. But coming at things from an unusual angle is as important to writing great essays as it is to the production of great poetry.

So, in summary, when reading a poem for the first time, such as when doing an 'unseen' style question, have a check list in mind, but don't feel you must follow someone else's generic essay recipe. Don't feel that you must always start with a consideration of imagery if the poem you're analysing has, for instance, an eye-catching form. Consider the significance of major features, such as imagery, vocabulary, sonic patterns and form. Try to write about these aspects in terms of their contribution to themes and effects. But also follow your nose, find your own direction, seek out aspects that genuinely engage you and write about these.

The essays in this volume provide examples and we hope they will encourage you to go your own way, at least to some extent, and to make discoveries for yourself. No single essay could possibly cover everything that could be said about any one of these poems; aiming to create comprehensive essays like this would be utterly foolish. And we have not tried to do so. Nor are our essays meant to be models for exam essays – they're far too long for that. They do, however, illustrate the sort of conceptualised, critical and 'fine-grained' exploration demanded for top grades at GCSE and beyond. There's always more to be discovered, more to say, space in other words for you to develop some original reading of your own, space for you to write your own individual essay recipe.

# Writing literature essays

### *The Big picture and the small*

An essay itself can be a form of art. And writing a great essay takes time, skill and practice. And also expert advice. Study the two figures in the picture carefully and describe what you can see. Channel your inner Sherlock Holmes to add any deductions you are able to form about the image. Before reading what we have to say, write your description out as a prose paragraph. Probably you'll have written something along the following lines:

First off, the overall impression: this picture is very blurry. Probably this indicates that either this is a very poor quality reproduction, or that it is a copy of a very small detail from a much bigger image that has been magnified several times. The image shows a stocky man and a medium-sized dog, both orientated towards something to their left, which suggests there is some point of interest in that direction. From the man's rustic dress (smock, breeches, clog-like boots) the picture is either an old one or a modern one depicting the past. The man appears to be carrying a stick and there's maybe a bag on his back. From all of these details we can probably deduce that he's a peasant, maybe a farmer or a shepherd.

Now do the same thing for picture two. We have even less detail here and again the picture's blurry. Particularly without the benefit of colour it's hard to determine what we're seeing other than a horizon and maybe the sky. We might just be able to make out that in the centre of the picture is the shape of the sun. From the reflection, we can deduce that the image is of the sun either setting or rising over water. If it is dawn this usually symbolises hope, birth and new beginnings; if the sun is setting it conventionally symbolises the opposite – the end of things, the coming of night/ darkness, death.

If you're a sophisticated reader, you might well start to think about links between the two images. Are they, perhaps, both details from the same single larger image, for instance.

Well, this image might be even harder to work out. Now we don't even have a
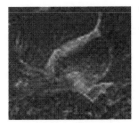
whole figure, just a leg, maybe, sticking up in the air. Whatever is happening here, it looks painful and we can't even see the top half of the body. From the upside orientation, we might guess that the figure is or has fallen. If we put this image with the one above, we might think the figure has fallen into water as there are horizontal marks on the image that could be splashes. From the quality of this image we can deduce that this is an even smaller detail blown-up.

You may be wondering by now why we've suddenly moved into rudimentary art appreciation. On the other hand, you may already have worked out the point of this exercise. Either way, bear with us, because this is the last picture for you to describe and analyse. So, what have we here? Looks like another peasant, again from the past, perhaps medieval (?) from the smock-like dress, clog-like shoes and the britches. This character is

also probably male and seems to be pushing some wooden apparatus from left to right. From the ridges at the bottom left of the image we can surmise that he's working the land, probably driving a plough. Noticeably the figure has his back to us; we see his turned away from us, suggesting his whole concentration is on the task at hand. In the background appear to be sheep, which would fit with our impression that this is an image of farming. It seems likely that this image and the first one come from the same painting. They have a similar style and subject and it is possible that these sheep belong to

our first character. This image is far less blurry than the other one. Either it is a better-quality reproduction, or this is a larger, more significant detail extracted from the original source. If this is a significant detail it's interesting that we cannot see the character's face. From this we can deduce that he's not important in and of himself; rather he's a representative figure and the important thing is what he is and what he isn't looking at.

Okay, we hope we haven't stretched your patience too far. What's the point of all this? Well, let's imagine we prefixed the paragraphs above with an introduction, along the following lines: 'The painter makes this picture interesting and powerful by using several key techniques and details' and that we added a conclusion, along the lines of 'So now I have shown how the painter has made this picture interesting and powerful through the use of a number of key techniques and details'. Finally, substitute painter and picture for writer and text. If we put together our paragraphs into an essay what would be its strengths and weaknesses? What might be a better way of writing our essay?

Consider the strengths first off. The best bits of our essay, we humbly suggest, are the bits where we begin to explain what we are seeing, when we do the Holmes like deductive thinking. Another strength might be that we have started to make links between the various images, or parts of a larger image, to see how they work together to provide us more information. A corresponding weakness is that each of our paragraphs seems like a separate chunk of writing. The weaker parts of the paragraphs are where we simply describe what we can see. More importantly though, if we used our comments on image one as our first paragraph we seem to have started in a rather random way. Why should we have begun our essay with that image? What was the logic behind that? And most importantly of all, if this image is an analogue for a specific aspect of a text, such as a poem's imagery or a novel's dialogue we have dived straight into to analysing this technical aspect before we're established any overall sense of the painting/ text. And this is a very common fault with GCSE English Literature essays. As we've said before and will keep saying, pupils start writing detailed micro-analysis of a detail such as alliteration before they have established the big picture of what the text is about and what the answer to the question they've been set might be. Without this big picture it's very difficult to write about the significance of the micro details. And the major marks for English essays are reserved for explanations of the significance and effects generated by a writer's craft.

Now we'll try a different and much better approach. Let's start off with the big picture, the whole image. The painting on the next page is called *Landscape with the fall of Icarus*. It's usually attributed to the Renaissance artist, Pieter Breughel and was probably painted in the 1560s. Icarus is a character from  Greek mythology. He was the son of the brilliant inventor, Daedalus. Trapped on Crete by the evil King Minos, Daedalus and Icarus managed to escape when the inventor created pairs of giant feathered wings. Before they took to sky Daedalus warned his son not to get too excited and fly too near the sun as the wings were held together by wax that might melt. Icarus didn't listen, however. The eventual result was that he plummeted back to earth, into the sea more precisely and was killed.

Applying this contextual knowledge to the painting we can see that the image is about how marginal Icarus' tragedy is in the big picture. Conventionally we'd expect any image depicting such a famous myth to make Icarus's fall the dramatic centre of attention. The main objects of this painting, however, are emphatically not the falling boy hitting the water. Instead our eye is drawn to the peasant in the centre of the painting, pushing his plough (even more so in colour as his shirt is the only red object in an otherwise greeny-yellow landscape) and the stately galleon sailing calmly past those protruding legs. Seeing the whole image, we can appreciate the significance of the shepherd and the ploughman looking up and down and to the left. The point being made is how they don't even notice the tragedy because they have work to do and need to get on with their lives. The animals too seem unconcerned. As W. H. Auden's puts it, in lines from *Musée des Beaux Arts*, 'everything turns away / Quite leisurely from the disaster'.

To sum up, when writing an essay on any literary text do not begin with close-up analysis of micro-details. Begin instead with establishing the whole picture: What the text is about, what key techniques the writer uses, when it was written, what sort of text it is, what effects it has on the reader. Then, when you zoom in to examine smaller details, such as imagery, individual words, metre or sonic techniques you can discuss these in relation to their significance in terms of this bigger picture.

What would our art appreciation essay look like now?

Paragraph #1: Introduction – myth of Icarus, date of painting, the way our eyes is drawn away from his tragic death to much more ordinary life going around him. Significance of this – even tragic suffering goes on around us without us even noticing, we're too busy getting on with our lives.

Paragraph #2: We could, of course, start with our first figure and follow the same order as we've presented the images here. But wouldn't it make more logical sense to discuss first the biggest, more prominent images in the painting first? So, our first paragraph is about the ploughman and his horse.

How his figure placed centrally and is bent downwards towards the ground and turned left away from us etc.

Paragraph #3: The next most prominent image is the ship. Also moving from right to left, as if the main point of interest in the painting is off in that direction. Here we could consider the other human agricultural figure, the shepherd and his dog and, of course, the equally oblivious sheep.

Paragraph #4: Having moved on to examining background details in the painting we could discuss the symbolism of the sun on the horizon. While this could be the sun rising, the context of the story suggests it is more likely to be setting. The pun of the sun/son going down makes sense.

Paragraph #5: Finally, we can turn our attention to the major historical and literary figure in this painting, Icarus and how he is presented. This is the key image in terms of understanding the painting's purpose and effect.

Paragraph #6: Conclusion. What is surprising about this picture. How do the choices the painter makes affect us as viewer/ reader? Does this painting make Icarus's story seem more pathetic, more tragic or something else?

Now, all you have to do is switch from a painting to a poem.

Big pictures, big cakes, recipes and lists of instructions; following your own nose and going your own way. Whatever metaphors we use, your task is to bring something personal and individual to your critical reading of poems and to your essay writing.

# Writing comparative essays

The following is adapted from our discussion of this topic in *The Art of Writing English Literature Essays* A-level course companion, and is a briefer version, tailored to the GCSE exam task. Fundamentally comparative essays want you to display not only your ability to intelligently talk about literary texts, but also your ability to make meaningful connections between them. The first starting point is your topic. This must be broad enough to allow substantial thematic overlapping of the texts. However, too little overlap and it will be difficult to connect the texts; too much overlap and your discussion will be lopsided and one-dimensional. In the case of the GCSE exam, the broad topics are likely to be conflict, the natural world or relationships. The exam question will ask you to focus on the methods used by the poets to explore how two poems present one of these themes. You will also be directed to write specifically on language and imagery [AO2] as well as on the contexts in which the poems were written [AO3].

One poem from the anthology will be specified and printed on the paper. You will then have to choose a companion poem. Selecting the right poem for interesting comparison is obviously very important. Obviously, you should prepare for this question beforehand by pairing up the poems, especially as you will only have about forty minutes to complete this task. You will also be asked to compare unseen poems, so grasping how best to write comparative essays is essential to your chance of reaching the top grades. To think about this task visually, you don't want Option A, below, [not enough overlap] or Option B [two much overlap]. You want Option C. This option allows substantial common links to be built between your chosen texts where discussion arises from both fundamental similarities AND differences.

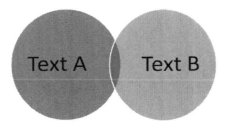

Option A: too many differences

Option B: too many similarities

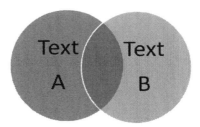

Option C: suitable number of similarities and differences

The final option will generate the most interesting discussion as it will allow substantial similarities to emerge as well as differences. <u>The best comparative essays actually find that what seemed like clear similarities become subtle differences and vice versa</u> while still managing to find rock solid similarities to build their foundations on.

Check the mark scheme for this question and you'll notice that to reach the top grade your comparison must be 'well-structured'. How should you structure a comparative essay? Consider the following alternatives. Which one is best and why?

Essay Structure #1
1. Introduction
2. Main body paragraph #1 - Text A
3. Main body paragraph #2 - Text A
4. Main body paragraph #3 - Text B
5. Main body paragraph #4 - Text B
6. Conclusion

Essay Structure #2
1. Introduction
2. Main body paragraph #1 - Text A
3. Main body paragraph #2 - Text A
4. Main body paragraph #3 - Text B
5. Main body paragraph #4 - Text B
6. Comparison of main body paragraphs #1 & #3 - Text A + B
7. Comparison of main body paragraphs #2 & #4 - Text A + B
8. Conclusion

Essay Structure #3
1. Introduction
2. Main body paragraph #1 - Text A + B
3. Main body paragraph #2 - Text A + B
4. Main body paragraph #3 - Text A + B
5. Main body paragraph #4 - Text A+ B
6. Conclusion

We hope you will agree that 3 is the optimum option. Option 1 is the dreaded 'here is everything I know about text A, followed by everything I know by Text B' approach where the examiner has to work out what the connections are between the texts. This will score the lowest marks. Option 2 is better: There is some attempt to compare the two texts. However, it is a very inefficient way of comparing the two texts. For comparative essay writing the most important thing is to discuss both texts together. This is the most effective and efficient way of achieving your overall aim. Option 3 does this by comparing and contrasting the two texts under common umbrella headings. This naturally encourages comparison. Using comparative discourse markers, such as 'similarly', 'in contrast to', 'conversely' 'likewise' and 'however' also facilitates effective comparison.

When writing about each poem, make sure you do not work chronologically through a poem, summarising the content of each stanza. Responses of this sort typically start with 'In the first stanza' and employ discourse markers of time rather than comparison, such as 'after', 'next', 'then' and so forth. Even if your reading is analytical rather than summative, your essay should not work through the poem from the opening to the ending. Instead, make sure you write about the ideas explored in both texts (themes), the feelings and effects generated and the techniques the poets utilise to achieve these.

# Writing about language

Poems are paintings as well as windows; we look at them as well as through them. As you know, special attention should be paid to language in poetry because of all the literary art forms poetry, in particular, employs language in a precise, self-conscious and distinctive way. Ideally in poetry, every word should count. Analysis of language falls into distinct categories:

- By diction we mean the vocabulary used in a poem. A poem might be composed from the ordinary language of everyday speech or it might use elaborate, technical or elevated phrasing. Or both. At one time, some words and types of words were considered inappropriate for the rarefied field of poetry. The great Irish poet, W. B. Yeats never referred to modern technology in his poetry, there are no cars, or tractors or telephones, because he did not consider such things fitting for poetry. When much later, Philip Larkin used swear words in his otherwise well-mannered verse the effect was deeply shocking. Modern poets have pretty much dispensed with the idea of there being an elevated literary language appropriate for poetry. Hence in the Eduqas anthology you'll find all sorts of modern, everyday language.

- Grammatically a poem may use complex or simple sentences [the key to which is the conjunctions]; it might employ a wash of adjectives and adverbs, or it may rely extensively on the bare force of nouns and verbs. Picking out and exploring words from specific grammatical classes has the merit of being both incisive and usually illuminating.

- Poets might mix together different types, conventions and registers of language, moving, for example, between formal and informal, spoken and written, modern and archaic, and so forth. Arranging the diction in the poem in terms of lexico-semantic fields, by register or by etymology, helps reveal underlying patterns of meaning.

- For almost all poems imagery is a crucial aspect of language. Broadly imagery is a synonym for description and can be broken down into two types, sensory and figurative. Sensory imagery means the words and phrases that appeal to our senses, to touch and taste, hearing, smell and sight. Sensory imagery is evocative; it helps to take us into the world of the poem to share the experience being described. Figurative imagery, in particular, is always significant. As we have mentioned, not all poems rely on metaphors and similes; these devices are only part of a poet's box of tricks, but figurative language is always important when it occurs because it compresses multiple meanings into itself. To use a technical term figurative images are polysemic - they contain many meanings. Try writing out the all the meanings contained in a metaphor in a more concise and economical way. Even simple, everyday metaphors compress meaning. If we want to say our teacher is fierce and powerful and that we fear his or her wrath, we can more concisely say our teacher is a dragon.

# Writing about patterns of sound

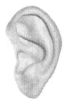 Like painters, some poets have powerful visual imaginations, while other poets have stronger auditory imaginations are more like musicians. And some poems are like paintings, others are more like pieces of music.

Firstly, what not to do: Tempting as it may be to spot sonic features of a poem and list these, don't do this. Avoid something along the lines of 'The poet uses alliteration here and the rhyme scheme is ABABCDCDEFEFGG'. Sometimes, indeed, it may be tempting to set out the poem's whole rhyme scheme like this. Resist the temptation: This sort of identification of features is worth zero marks. Marks in exams are reserved for attempts to link techniques to meanings and to effects.

Probably many of us have been sitting in English lessons listening somewhat sceptically as our English teacher explains the surprisingly specific significance of a seemingly random piece of alliteration in a poem. Something along the lines 'The double d sounds here reinforce a sense of invincible strength' or 'the harsh repetition of the 't' sounds suggests anger'. Through all our minds at some point may have passed the idea that, in these instances, English teachers appear to be using some sort of Enigma-style secret symbolic decoding machine that reveals how particular patterns of sounds have such definite encoded meanings.

And this sort of thing is not all nonsense. Originally deriving from an oral tradition, poems are, of course, written for the ear as much as for the eye, to be heard as much as read. A poem is a soundscape as much as it is a set of meanings. Sounds are, however, difficult to tie to very definite meanings and effects. By way of example, the old BBC Radiophonic workshop, which produced ambient sounds for radio and television programmes, used the same sounds in different contexts, knowing that the audience would perceive them in the appropriate way because of that context. Hence the sound of bacon sizzling, of an audience clapping and of feet walking over gravel were actually recordings of an identical sound. Listeners heard them differently because of the context. So, we may, indeed, be able to spot the repeated 's' sounds in a poem, but whether this creates a hissing sound, yes like a snake, or the susurration of the sea will depend on the context within the poem and the ears of the reader. Whether a sound is soft and soothing or harsh and grating is also open to interpretation.

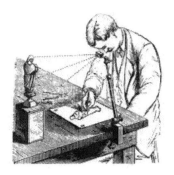

The idea of connecting these sounds to meanings or significance is a productive one. And your analysis will be most convincing if you use several pieces of evidence together. In other words, rather than try to pick out individual examples of sonic effects we recommend you explore the weave or pattern of sounds, the effects these generate and their contribution to feelings and ideas. For example, this might mean examining how alliteration and assonance are used together to achieve a particular mimetic effect.

# Writing about form & structure

As you know, there are no marks for simply identifying textual features. This holds true for language, sounds and also for form. Consider instead the relationship between a poem's form and its content, themes and effects. Form is not merely decorative or ornamental: A poem's meanings and effects are generated through the interplay of form and content. Broadly speaking the form can either work with or against a poem's content. Conventionally a sonnet, for instance, is about love, whereas a limerick is a comic form. A serious love poem in the form of a limerick would be unusual, as would a sonnet about an old man with a beard.

Sometimes poetic form can create an ironic backdrop to highlight an aspect of content. An example would be a formally elegant poem about something

monstrous, or a fragile form containing something robust. Owen's double sonnet, *Dulce et Decorum Est* or Dharker's *Living Space* might spring to mind. The artist Grayson Perry uses form in this ironic way. Rather than depicting the sort of picturesque, idealised images we expect of ceramics, Perry's pots and urns depict modern life in bright, garish colours. The urn pictured, for instance, is entitled *Modern Family* and depicts two gay men with a boy who they have presumably adopted. A thrash metal concert inside a church, a philosophical essay via text message, a fine crystal goblet filled with cherryade would be further examples of ironic relationships between message and medium, content and context or form.

********

### Reading form

Put a poem before your eyes. Start off taking a panoramic perspective: Think of the forest, not the trees. Perhaps mist over your eyes a bit. Don't even read the words, just look at the poem, like at a painting. Is the poem slight, thin, fat, long, short? What is the relation of whiteness to blackness? Why might the poet have chosen this shape? Does it look regular or irregular? A poem about a long winding river will probably look rather different from one about a small pebble, or should do. Unless form is being employed ironically. Now read the poem a couple of times. First time, fast as you can, second time more slowly and carefully. How does the visual layout of the poem relate to what it seems to be about? Does this form support, or create a tension against, the content? Is the form one you recognise, like a sonnet, or is it more open, more irregular like free verse? Usually the latter is obvious from the irregularity of the stanzas, line lengths and lack of metre or rhyme.

As Hurley and O'Neill explain in *Poetic Form: An Introduction*, like genre, form sets expectations: 'In choosing form, poets bring into play associations and expectations which they may then satisfy, modify or subvert'.[1] We've already suggested that if we see a poem is a sonnet or a limerick this recognition will set up expectations about the nature of the poem's content. The same thing works on a smaller level; once we have noticed that a poem's first stanza is a quatrain, we expect it to continue in this neat, orderly fashion. If the quatrain's rhyme scheme is xaxa, xbxb, in which only the second and fourth lines rhyme, we reasonably expect that the next stanza will be xcxc. So, if it isn't we need to consider why.

After taking in the big picture in terms of choice of form in relation to content zoom in: Explore the stanza form, lineation, punctuation, the use of enjambment and caesura. Single line stanzas draw attention to themselves. If they are end-stopped they can suggest isolation, separation. Couplets imply twoness. Stanzas of three lines are called tercets and feature in villanelles and terza rima. On the page, both these forms tend to look rather delicate, especially if separated from each other by the silence of white space. Often balanced through rhyme, quatrains look a bit more robust and sturdy. Cinquains are swollen quatrains in which the last line often seems to throw the stanza out of balance.

---

[1] Hurley & O'Neill, *Poetic Form, An Introduction*, p.3

Focus in on specific examples and on points of transition. For instance, if a poem has four regular quatrains followed by a couplet, examine the effect of this change. If we've been ticking along nicely in iambic metre and suddenly trip on a trochee, examine why. Consider regularity. Closed forms of poems, such as sonnets, are highly regular with set rhyme schemes, metre and number of lines. The opposite form is called 'open', the most extreme version of which is free verse. In free verse poems, the poet dispenses with any set metre, rhyme scheme or recognisable traditional form. What stops this sort of poetry from being prose chopped up to look like verse? The care of the design on the page. Hence, we need to focus here on lineation. Enjambment runs over lines and makes connections; caesura pauses a line and separates words. Lots of enjambment generates a sense of the language running away from the speaker. Lots of caesuras generate a halting, hesitant, choppy movement to lines. Opposites, these devices work in tandem and where they fall is always significant in a good poem.

Remember poetic form is never merely decorative. And bear in mind too the fact that the most volatile materials require the strongest containers.

# *Nice to metre...*

# A brief guide to metre and rhythm in poetry

Why express yourself in poetry? Why read words dressed up and expressed as a poem? What can you get from poetry that you can't from prose? There are many compelling answers to these questions. Here, though, we're going to concentrate on one aspect of the unique appeal of poetry – the structure of sound in poetry. Whatever our stage of education, we are all already sophisticated at detecting and using structured sound. Try reading the following sentences without any variation whatsoever in how each sound is

 emphasised, and they will quickly lose what essential human characteristics they

have. The sentences will sound robotic. So, in a sense, we won't be teaching anything new here. It's just that in poetry the structure of sound is carefully unusually crafted and created. It becomes a key part of what a poem is.

We will introduce a few new key technical terms along the way, but the ideas are straightforward. Individual sounds [syllables] are either stressed [emphasised, sounding louder and longer] or unstressed. As well as clustering into words and sentences for meaning, these sounds [syllables] cluster into rhythmic groups or feet, producing the poem's metre, which is the characteristic way its rhythm works.

In some poems, the rhythm is very regular and may even have a name, such as iambic pentameter. At the other extreme a poem may have no discernible regularity at all. As we have said, this is called free verse. It is vital to remember that the sound in a good poem is structured so that it combines effectively with the meanings.

For example, take a look at these two lines from Marvell's *To his Coy Mistress*:

'But at my back I alwaies hear
Times winged Chariot hurrying near:'

Forgetting the rhythms for a moment, Marvell is basically saying at this point 'Life is short, Time flies, and it's after us'. Now concentrate on the rhythm of his words.

- In the first line every other syllable is stressed: 'at', 'back', 'al', 'hear'.
- Each syllable before these is unstressed 'But', 'my', 'I', 'aies'.
- This is a regular beat or rhythm which we could write
  ti TUM / ti TUM / ti TUM / ti TUM , with the / separating the feet. ['Feet' is the technical term for metrical units of sound]
- This type of two beat metrical pattern is called iambic, and because there are four feet in the line, it is tetrameter. So this line is in 'iambic tetrameter'. [Tetra is Greek for four]
- Notice that 'my' and 'I' being unstressed diminishes the speaker, and we are already prepared for what is at his 'back', what he can 'hear' to be bigger than him, since these sounds are stressed.
- On the next line, the iambic rhythm is immediately broken off, since the next line hits us with two consecutive stressed syllables straight off: 'Times' 'wing'. Because a pattern had been established, when it suddenly changes the reader feels it, the words feel crammed together more urgently, the beats of the rhythm are closer, some little parcels of time have gone missing.

A physical rhythmic sensation is created of time slipping away, running out. This subtle sensation is enhanced by the stress-unstress-unstress pattern of words that follow, 'chariot hurrying' [TUM-ti-ti, TUM-ti-ti]. So the hurrying sounds underscore the meaning of the words.

# 14 ways of looking at a poem

 Though conceived as pre-reading exercises, most of these tasks work just as well for revision.

1. Mash them (1) – mix together lines from two or more poems. The students' task is to untangle the poems from each other.

2. Mash them (2) – the second time round make the task significantly harder. Rather than just mixing whole lines, mash the poems together more thoroughly, words, phrases, images and all, so that unmashing seems impossible. At first sight.

3. Dock the last stanza or few lines from a poem. The students should come up with their own endings for the poem. Compare with the poet's version. Or present the poem without its title. Can the students come up with a suitable one?

4. Break a poem into segments. Split the class into groups. Each group work in isolation on their segment and feedback on what they discover. Then their task is to fit the poem and their ideas about it together as a whole.

5. Give the class the first and last stanza of a poem. Their task is to provide the filling. They can choose to attempt the task at beginner level (in prose) or at world class level (in poetry).

6. Add superfluous words to a poem. Start off with obvious interventions, such as the interjection of blatantly alien, noticeable words. Try smuggling 'pineapple', 'bourbon' and 'haberdashers' into any of the poems and see if you can get it past the critical sensors.

7. Repeat the exercise – This time using much less extravagant words. Try to smuggle in a few intensifiers, such as 'really', 'very' and 'so'. Or extra adjectives.

8. Collapse the lineation in a poem and present it as continuous prose. The students' task is to put it back into verse. Discussing the various pros and cons or various possible arrangements – short lines, long lines, irregular lines - can be very productive. Pay particular attention to line breaks and the words that end them. After a whatever-time-you-deem-fit, give the class the pattern of the first stanza. They then have to decide how to arrange the next stanza. Drip feed the rest of the poem to them.

9. Find a way to present the shapes of each poem on the page without the words. The class should work through each poem, two minutes at a time, speculating on what the shape might tell us about the content of the poem. This exercise works especially well as a starter activity. We recommend you use two poems at a time, as the comparison helps students to recognise and appreciate different shapes.

10. Test the thesis that an astute reader can recognise poems by men from those written by women. Give the class one of the poems, such as *Sonnet 43 or Living Space*, without the name of the poet. Ask them to identify whether the writer is male or female and to explain their reasons for identifying them as such.

11. Split the class into groups. Each group should focus their analysis on a different feature of the poem. Start with the less obvious aspects: Group 1 should concentrate on enjambment and caesuras; group 2 on punctuation; group 3 on the metre and rhythm; group 4 on function words – conjunctions, articles, prepositions. 2-5 mins. only. Then swap focus, four times. Share findings.

12. In ***Observations on Poetry***, Robert Graves wrote that 'rhymes properly used are the good servants whose presence at the dinner-table gives the guests a sense of opulent security; never awkward or over-clever, they hand the dishes silently and professionally. You can trust them not to interrupt the conversation or allow their personal disagreements to come to the notice of the guests; but some of them are getting very old for their work'. Explore the poets' use of rhyme in the light of Graves' comment. Are the rhymes ostentatiously original or old hat? Do they stick out of the poem or are they neatly tucked in? Are they dutiful servants of meaning or noisy disrupters of the peace?

13. The Romantic poet, John Keats, claimed that 'we hate poetry that has a palpable design upon us – and if we do not agree seems to put its hand its breeches pock'. Apply his comment to this selection of poems. Do any seem to have a 'palpable design' on the reader? If so, how does the poet want us to respond?

14. Each student should crunch the poem down to one word per line. Discuss this process as a class. Project the poem so the whole class can see it and start the crunching process by indicating and then crossing-out the function words from each line. Now discuss which of the remaining words is most important. This will also give you an opportunity to refer to grammatical terms, such as nouns and verbs. Once each line has been reduced to one word, from this list, pupils should crunch again. This time all that should remain are the five most important words in the whole poem. Now they need to write two or three sentences for each of these words explaining exactly why they are so important and why the poet didn't choose any of the possible synonyms.

'Poetry is only there to frame the silence. There is silence between each verse and silence at the end.'

ALICE OSWALD

# Simon Armitage, *The Manhunt*

## War poetry

The most famous and celebrated war poets tend to be those who experienced combat first-hand. For unforgettable, visceral descriptions of WWI we turn to writers such as Wilfred Owen and Siegfried Sassoon. Probably the most celebrated WWII poet is Keith Douglas who, like Owen, was killed in action. The fact that these poets were first-hand witnesses to the horrors of war lends their poetry the potency of testimony. If you are a modern poet who has never been a soldier and has never fought in a battle, you might well hesitate and consider carefully before trying to write a war poem. Readers might believe only those who have direct experience of war can describe it; for a civilian to try this would be at best an act of crass insensitivity and at worst of tasteless appropriation, in effect a stealing of other people's experience. It's not then without trepidation that a poet as self-aware as Simon Armitage would choose such a difficult subject.

And by all accounts, Armitage did not only rely on the power of his own imagination. Instead he conducted many interviews with soldiers and their partners before writing poems that contributed to a moving television documentary for Channel 4 about returning war veterans, called *The Not Dead*. You can hear him talking about this process as well as a poignant reading of *The Manhunt* at: www.youtube.com/watch?v=TtDiOsQsnRw. Here the poet talks about the responsibility he felt in writing about real people's lives, 'real people who had been involved in conflicts where people had been injured and died and who have killed people as well'.

## A sweating, unexploded mine

This context helps explain Armitage's decision not to write in the voice of the soldier himself. Instead he chooses to compose this dramatic monologue in the voice of a partner, perhaps the soldier's wife. <u>What is the effect of this choice of narration?</u> The most important one, I think, is that it results in the soldier

remaining silent; we never hear his voice or his version of what happened to him. This means he remains something of a mystery to us, we only view him from the outside and through the eyes of his partner; we have no access to his private thoughts. In this sense, he is lost to us as readers in an analogous way to how he is lost to his partner, a kind of blank we try to fill. The hunt of the title is her attempt to 'find' him. As readers we are engaged in this 'hunt' too. For some soldiers a symptom of what used to be called shellshock was mutism and for many soldiers, in many wars, it has been difficult or impossible to talk about their traumatic experiences. Making the soldier the subject of the poem, but not its narrator, also helps establish him as an everyman figure, standing in for all damaged combatants in all wars. Hence this soldier's silence has a greater, wider, more poignant resonance.

What we do learn about him is how his body has been horribly damaged by war. The poem presents him as a series of wrecked body parts, a collection of broken pieces that have to be put together gently and carefully in order to try to reconstruct the whole person he once was. A 'frozen river' runs 'through his face'; his jaw is a 'blown hinge'; his should-blade is a 'fractured rudder'. Every fragmentary piece of him is itself also 'broken', 'grazed' or scarred. Usually comparing somebody to objects, such as hinges and rudders, dehumanises them. And we would expect this to lead us to feel less sympathy - it's harder for us to care about things rather than people, normally. But here, Armitage manages to make his metaphors have the reverse effect, generating greater sympathy. Maybe this is because they imply that the soldier himself feels dehumanised, just an assemblage of mechanical bits and parts. Worse, though she is expressing tenderness towards him, it seems that his partner now also sees him in this dehumanised way.

Arguably the instances of physical injury to the outer self are less significant than the emotional and psychological damage to his inner self. Hinges can be fixed, rudders put back together, rivers can unfreeze. Nursing the inner person back to health will probably be more difficult, a fact acknowledged by the way the partner starts by trying to ease the physical suffering. Slowly this allows her to work towards discovering, and then dealing with, the locked away and buried mental trauma. How, for instance, do you treat a 'grazed heart', a heart that has been hurt and maybe now finds it difficult to express love? How do you minister to a mind which has buried within it the capacity for explosive, annihilating destruction? With great care and patience.

## Only then

This is the difficult, delicate and perhaps dangerous task facing the poem's speaker. She describes herself as like an explorer moving stealthily over potentially hostile territory in search of a clue, or first cause or 'source', something, anything that will allow them to reach the soldier mentally and emotionally and help him deal with his trauma. One hesitant step at a time, 'climbing' and 'skirting along', the narrator is allowed to 'trace' and 'explore' and 'search'. Alongside the language of exploration runs the language of nursing. The speaker tells us how she tries to 'handle and hold', 'mind and attend', 'bind'

and 'feel the hurt'. She operates with great tenderness, seen especially in her delicate descriptions of her partner's collar-bone and lungs as fragile 'porcelain' and fine 'silk' respectively. Though with its emphasis on touch, the language conveys a sense of physical, loving intimacy, at the same time there is a sense of a distance, of an inner core of his pain that is difficult to reach.

Repetition of the phrase 'only then' is significant. Appearing five times in the poem, mostly at the starts of lines, it conveys the tense delicacy of her actions. At each stage of slowly increasing intimacy the speaker must wait until it is safe, as if for permission, before she can move onwards and inwards. As if, at any stage, or at any false move, the alarm bells of his defences might go off and she might be prevented from going any further. Or worse might happen. It is like she is moving through a series of locked doors, or over a booby-trapped landscape or creeping past watchtowers. Each time she must unlock the door through touch, defuse the potential explosive through love and then take the next careful step on her journey, onwards, inwards. Commas at the ends of these lines add to the sense of the pauses taken before the speaker moves forwards. 'Hypervigilance' is another form of PTSD in which the sufferer develops an extreme and obsessive sensitivity to possible threats. The sufferer cannot relax; they are constantly on guard. Touching her partner's body, the speaker must be incredibly wary; she must not be perceived as a potential threat.

The access she is allowed increases as the poem progresses. At first, for instance, the phrase 'only then' is succeeded by 'would he let me', highlighting the need for his permission before she can continue. The three similarly structured stanzas, numbers 4,5 and 6, all beginning the simplest conjunction 'and', suggest that, essentially, in each of these the speaker is doing variations of the same thing, tracing his wounds. But that repetition allows the soldier to get used to the tactile intimacy, perhaps even to drop his guard a bit, perhaps even relax a little, so that by the seventh couplet there is progress. From here on in all the remaining 'only thens' are succeeded by her actions – 'could I', 'did I'.

The poem's form contributes to the sense of tentative development. Irregular, unmetred, it is impossible to predict the length of the lines in each couplet.

Hence the form of the poem is akin to the speaker feeling her way, working out what to do as she goes along. Or we could relate the form to the soldier. Judged from the outside he might appear fine. But that outer order would only hide the disorder within. But this inner uncertainty, hers, his or both, is contained within the  consistent use of the couplet form. At no time does this form break down. It holds and it endures. The use of rhyme also holds out the possibility of harmony, as rhyme is a form of sonic resolution, of words fitting together musically. It's significant, then, that not all the couplets rhyme and the overall pattern of the poem is towards looser rhymes. Compare, for example, the opening rhymes, 'phase/ days' and 'trace/ face' with the end words in the last two couplets, 'mine/ which' and 'closed/ close'. Read pessimistically, this loosening could suggest that the couple are not, in fact, getting closer together as the poem develops. Read optimistically, however, the loosening of the tight rhyme pattern might signal the easing of tension. This central ambiguity itself generates further tension for the reader.

Simon Armitage himself has suggested that a helpful way in to analysing a poem is to pick about five words that interest you as a reader and to put these words under the microscope. There's a word in this poem that immediately leaps out at me. It leaps out because it seems incongruous, completely out of place in this context. That word is 'foetus'. Describing the fragment of a bullet buried in the man's chest as a 'foetus' is an extraordinary thing to do. Why? Because normally we associate seeing a foetus within a body with women, with pregnancy and with childbirth. When parents-to-be first see the image of their foetus it is normally an incredibly happy and humbling moment in their lives. A foetus = new life, new beginnings, new hope for the future. In this man's chest the image is unnatural and almost monstrous. Bringing the reader up short, it very powerfully conveys the idea that his damage is growing within him and at some point will fully develop and be released.

39

## Enduring love

Noticeably Armitage chose some very similar words close together at the end of the poem. Normally such repetition is frowned upon in prose narrative, especially when it could easily have been avoided through the use of synonyms. For example, the poet could easily have referred to the 'mine' as being buried deep in the soldier's 'head' or 'brain' or 'thoughts'. But, instead he chose 'mind'. Similarly, in the penultimate and final line he could have used 'shut', instead of 'closed', or 'near', instead of 'close'. So, why didn't he avoid this clumsiness? What does he gain? The sonic closeness between 'mine' and 'mind' signals that the former has nearly filled up the latter. The soldier's mind has almost become a mine. This connection is cemented using the adjective 'sweating'. Applied to and personifying the inanimate 'mine', it collapses the distinction between it and the soldier. In a profound sense the soldier himself has become 'a sweating, unexploded mine' that could go off at any time. Armitage's poems ends with the speaker not quite having reached the heart of the trauma. As she gets closest to the 'source' the soldier tenses up again: 'every nerve in his body had tightened'. The doors she had opened in him are now suddenly 'closed'. In this context, her coming 'close' could imply that she failed, she missed. However, the use of almost an identical word as first a verb and then an adjective, to describe first his action and then hers, suggests another more optimistic reading. The sharing of this final word is like the consistent use of the couplet form. It implies shared experience, a mutuality the couple share, something that, despite everything, will endure.

*The Manhunt* crunched:

**FIRST – INTIMATE – ONLY – FROZEN – EXPLORE – BLOWN – HOLD – DAMAGED – MIND – RUDDER – FINGER – SILK – BIND – BROKEN – FEEL – GRAZED – SKIRTING – THEN – FOETUS – BULLET – SEARCH – MINE – DEEP – CLOSED – CLOSE**

# Elizabeth Barrett Browning, *Sonnet 43*

## A modest disguise

Elizabeth Barrett Browning wrote *Sonnet 43* as a private expression of her love for fellow poet Robert Browning, with whom she had begun a secret courtship. The couple later married, but her wealthy father disowned her as he did not approve of her choice. It was only after they eloped and were married that Elizabeth mentioned she had written a series of sonnets about her husband while they were courting. When Robert read them, he thought they were the best sonnets written in English since Shakespeare's and encouraged her to publish. However, they were so personal and revealing, having never been intended for anyone other than Elizabeth Barrett Browning herself, that they were published under the title *Sonnets from the Portuguese*, in an attempt to pretend they were obscure translations of another poet, rather than intimate expressions of her own private emotions. Some of the sonnets, such as *Sonnet 29,* are intensely personal and express a love that is passionate and erotic. *Sonnet 43*, in contrast, conveys a more spiritual, devotional and platonic sort of love. Nevertheless, the reader is given unusually intimate access to the poet's private feelings.

## Breadth and depth and height

The short opening question immediately creates a sense of a private conversation, as if the poet is responding to this question. The language is noticeably very simple. In the first line all the words are common monosyllables and they are employed in a literal way within two short sentences that also have straightforward syntax. Such simplicity is testament to the honesty and truth of what the poet is saying; there is no need for her to dress up, inflate, disguise or aggrandise her feelings through metaphor or symbolism. Her language is direct, unvarnished and as transparent as water.

In the following lines, however, similarly simple words are used in a more complex, figurative way. Barrett Browning employs a spatial metaphor for the soul and imagines the furthest limits it could stretch - to its utmost 'depth and  breadth and height'. Such is the love she feels that it fills her whole soul. Moreover it reaches even into unknown dimensions ['feelings out of sight'], to furthermost extent of her 'being' and echoes the very best of herself, 'ideal grace'. And this is a poem very much of the soul. The heart, that traditional symbol of love, does not even get a single mention. Instead the poem expresses a spiritual, disembodied, idealised love. Hence the religious touchstones of 'grace', 'faith', 'saints' and 'God'.

If this version of love seems impossibly idealistic, rarefied and saintly, Barrett Browning strikes a less elevated note in the following lines. Bringing the poem down to a more ordinary pitch, she refers to the everyday and to what we 'need'. Again, the superlative implies deepest, spiritual needs, rather than more clamorous cravings or desires. The upright, good and virtuous aspect of this love is then developed. The poet associates her love with the universal progressive fight for justice, and praises its resistance to the allurements of ego and vanity. At this point in the poem we have reached the end of the opening eight lines, or octave. Barrett Browning's sonnet follows the Petrarchan form [from the Italian poet Petrarch, depicted below] with a rhyme scheme of ABBA ABBA CDC DCD. Technically this is a particularly difficult version of the sonnet to handle in English because the whole construct has only four rhyme sounds, ABCD.

Shakespeare's version of the sonnet, in contrast, almost doubled the number of rhyme sounds to seven, making an Elizabethan sonnet considerably easier to write [though that's only in relative terms, of course]. The fact that Barrett Browning achieves this octave with such grace and apparent lack of effort – the words sound natural despite having to fit such a tight pattern, makes it correlate to the ideal love expressed. The form of the poem not only fits but expresses its meaning. However, a

Petrarchan sonnet has a 'volta' between the eighth and ninth lines. Conventionally sonnets have a call and response, or question and answer structure, with the sestet [final six lines] responding to something proposed in the octave. A volta marks a turn in the subject of a sonnet, sometimes signalled with a 'but' or 'however' or similar signposts for a switch in perspective.

Look for the volta in *Sonnet 43* and you'll not be able to find it. This is because despite our expectations that they must come, no counterarguments to the propositions set out in the octave appear. Instead the poem runs straight over and continues expressing the same loving sentiments, only in new ways. The first line of the sestet, for instance, begins with exactly the same phrase, 'I love thee' as the previous two lines of the octave have done, and overall this simple phrase is repeated four times in both halves of the poem. Hence the whole the depth and breadth and height of the sonnet is itself filled with Barrett Browning's ideal love.

## To perfection and beyond

After the references to faith, grief and faith, the poet finishes her sonnet with language that is simple, unadorned and poignant:

'I love thee with the breath/ smiles, tears of all my life'

Moreover, such a love, she tells us, will not only transcend death, it will become immortal. Perfect though it already is, it will also be refined by death.

The danger with such a restrained and graceful expression of such an elevated, ideal love is that it will feel overly chaste and bloodless; it may seem a love more suitable for angels than for thinking, feeling, imperfect human beings. Though there is a reference to 'passion', this is not the fiery or dangerous passions of erotic or sensual love. Rather it is passion in terms of strong and earnest feelings. There is a little sense of excited agitation in the lines quoted above, created by the quickening run of unstressed syllables and the tripartite list, 'breath, smiles, tears'. But perhaps we need to read some of the other sonnets to find the real passion in Barrett Browning's love for Robert. It is surely significant that this poem is the penultimate one in the series of sonnets, the culmination and zenith of the sequence.

As readers, we are placed in the position of the beloved. We are addressed directly as 'thee' and this rather archaic, perhaps timeless, pronoun is used in almost every line. How would you feel if someone said all this to you? How might Robert have felt? Delighted? Flattered? Daunted? All of these? Perhaps you might like to write his response, in either letter or verse form:

'*Dearest Lizzie,*

*I read your poem and I am moved beyond words can express...*'

Broadly speaking, historically, sonnets were most often written by men. Frequently they were love poems, often about, and addressed to, women. Women in sonnets tended to objectified, sometimes even deified as goddesses. So, conventionally the sonnet was a form in which men could show off their wit and write something seductive. Barrett Browning colonises the predominantly male poetic space of the sonnet and demonstrates that she can too handle the form. And, Robert was surely right in thinking that his wife could writes sonnets with just as much panache and variety as any male writer. In this sense, her sonnets can be read from a feminist perspective. Barrett Browning's sonnets equal, or indeed, surpass male artistic achievements in the form [apart from Shakespeare, perhaps]. In addition, her role as a sonneteer, boldly expressing her love for a male 'object' reflects the loosening of rigid Victorian concepts of gender and the great advances made by women towards the end of the age.

*Sonnet 43* crunched:

**HOW – LOVE – SOUL – IDEAL – EVERY – NEED – FREELY – PURELY – PASSION – FAITH – LOSE – SAINTS – GOD - BETTER**

# William Blake, *London*

The first thing to notice about Blake's poem is its burning anger. Written over two hundred years ago, the nightmare vision of this poem still seems irradiated with the poet's righteous fury. Fury at the corruption London's inhabitants had to endure, fury at the powers maintaining and enforcing this corruption. And who or what is to blame for the universal corruption? Blake is characteristically direct and bold: The finger of blame is pointed at commerce, the church and the monarchy.

Land and water in this poem have both been 'chartered', an adjective that indicates that they have become property, to be bought and sold by chartered companies. However, Blake subtly implies a potential counter force; the verb 'flows', with its slight echo of 'wander', perhaps implies that the river at least has the potential to escape its commercial restriction. For Blake, the Church was part of a corrupt, oppressive state. Here the churches are 'black'ning' because they should be an active voice of protest against the exploitation of children. The failure of the church blackens its name as well as its bricks. The blood of the soldier runs down the palace walls, a gruesome symbol of the sacrifice the ordinary man makes for King and country.

## Every voice

Repetition is a key poetic device for all poets, but it is especially important for Blake. It can fall into a few different categories: diction (or vocabulary); syntax (word order); images; sounds.

- In *London* there are lots of 'ins', 'ands', 'everys' as well as 'chartered', 'marks' and 'cry'.
- As well as repetition of single words there is repetition of syntax: 'in every...in every...in every'.
- Sound patterns are also repeated, such as in 'marks of weakness, marks of woe', 'mind-forg'd manacles', 'most through midnight', 'blasts' and 'blights'.
- Most importantly images are also repeated: The images of the chimney sweep, the soldier and the prostitute are three versions of the same figure; the character marginalized and exploited by society.

As well as creating rhetorical emphasis and a powerful rhythmical charge, reminiscent of spells and incantations, such insistent repetition creates an almost claustrophobic sound world, one that is an aural equivalent of the oppression Blake is describing.

The poem's rhyme scheme is cross-rhyme in quatrains: ABAB, CDCD and so forth. All the rhymes are masculine, a choice that also contributes to the peculiar intensity of the poem. For example, in the fourth line the stress starts with a strong stress on 'marks' and ends with another strong stress on 'woe'. Each stanza constitutes one sentence, completed in its final emphatic monosyllable. Metre, rhyme, diction, lineation and syntax all work together to amass maximum weight and stress on these last key words, 'woe', 'hear', 'walls' and finally, of course, 'hearse'.

The poem comprises four stanzas of four lines (quatrains) each with four beats. This consistency creates a concentration, further adding to its power. Structurally the poem also increases in intensity, as we move from verbs such as 'flow' and 'mark' in the first stanza to the more powerful emphatic 'curse', 'blasts' and 'blights' in the final stanza. As we go on to examine, this pattern is re-enforced by the increasingly poignant examples of exploitation, from the general populace to the chimney sweeper to the 'youthful harlot' whose curse Blake hears 'most'.

## The dark mark

As in fellow poet William Wordsworth's famous 'I wander lonely as a cloud', 'wander' is a form of motion particularly associated with Romanticism. Wandering suggests freedom, finding one's own path, without any specific aim in mind. It may also imply a sense of being lost. In Blake's poem, the verb emphasizes the idea that exploitation in London is universal; the poet doesn't have to search for it, whatever direction he takes he's sure to find it. Though they are in the active voice, the verbs connected to the narrator – 'wander', 'mark', 'hear' - suggest that Blake is passive and perhaps powerless. Rather than an active participant in the world of the poem who can make things happen, he is an outsider, a witness, registering his impressions as vividly as he can. Perhaps this is the role of the artist.

However, look at the line: 'and mark in every face I meet/ marks of weakness, marks of woe'. 'Mark' is used here first as a verb and then as a noun, and is a word connecting the narrator to the suffering people. Blake could easily have chosen a different verb. He was an engraver as well as a poet and to engrave the pictures that accompanied the poems in *Songs of Innocence and Experience* he would have had to cut into metal. Compared to 'see' or 'notice', 'mark' signals permanence. It also implies something doomed, as in the mark of Cain, or for Harry Potter fans the 'dark mark'. The fact that the poet 'marks' the people's 'marks' implies an equality and connection between them. If he is an outsider, he's an insider too, expressing a radical sympathy with the suffering he sees.

Repetition of the adjective 'every' emphasizes Blake's idea that every human being matters. The crowd represents the ordinary masses, the common people, whose suffering is often ignored by those in power. Over in France,

Europe's leaders had witnessed the first 'successful' rebellion of the commoners in history. The British government responded with a harsh crackdown on freedom. Romantic poets often sided with people marginalised by society or oppressed by authority; Blake's poem protests against the malign effects of power on those at the bottom of society. The soldier, sweep and prostitute are emblems of exploitation: The sweep would have been a young boy sold into a form of slavery (see Blake's two Chimney Sweeper poems in *Songs of Innocence and Experience*). Abused and brutalised, sweeps were regarded at this time as the lowest form of human life, on a par with 'savages' who shared their black skin. The soldier's blood is used to protect the state and the monarchy. The prostitute is, however, an example of the worst possible exploitation. Blake believed love to be sacred. Turning sex and love into a commodity to be bought and sold was therefore a sin against God, the most heinous form of sacrilege.

This is a poem full of aural as well as visual imagery: The voices of the Londoners, the clink of their mental manacles, the cries of the sweepers, the cursing of the prostitute. For Romantic Poets, such as Blake, nature was sacred. Nature manifested God on earth and was a great source of poetic inspiration. This unhappy, discordant, diseased, corrupted city is the nightmare opposite of Eden. The image of the soldier's 'sigh'

running in 'blood down palace walls' combines sound with sight. It is extraordinary in two ways: firstly, Blake transforms sound, a 'sigh', into something visual. The synaesthetic effect generated has a nightmarish quality; secondly, as we have already noted, he bravely points directs the blame at the King. This was a very dangerous thing to say in England in 1792, in a time when some of Blake's fellow radicals were being arrested by the government and attacked by pro monarchy gangs. The penalties for treason were very severe.

## Thought control

The 'mind forg'd manacles' is one of Blake's most
celebrated images. It is characteristically Blakean
because it conveys an idea (here of being
brainwashed) in a concrete, physical image. The image of the manacles is
one of mental chains, thought control, indoctrination. The poet does not
indicate who forges these manacles. It could be that they are made by the
state through propaganda. But they could also be formed in the minds of
individuals, in their blinkered perceptions and ways of seeing the world. In
either case, there is hope - these aren't real chains; they are 'mind forg'd' and
perceptions can be changed, perhaps by poetry. 'Forg'd' is a doubly
appropriate verb: An image drawn from metal work, it is a pun. These
perceptions of reality are forgeries, forgeries that can and must be exposed by
the sort of truth articulated in this poem.

Arguably, however, the poem's most potent image is the final one. Notice how
the structure of the poem develops in a cinematic fashion. Starting with the
equivalent of an establishing shot - a wide-angle image of the landscape, the
focus narrows to a closer in inspection of the crowds, and finishes with a shot
of a single emblematic figure. Like a film camera we sweep the whole scene
then zoom in as day darkens to night, before finishing, seemingly inevitably at
the apex of exploitation, the moral midnight of the 'youthful harlot'.

Blake employs an image of sexual infection as a metaphor for moral
corruption. Disease spreads through time and space: It will be spread through
the generations, from the prostitute to her child; spread from prostitute to
client, and spread into marriage, the home, the family. The deadly destruction
this process will wreak is conveyed by those violent plosive & alliterative verbs
'blasts' and the biblical 'blights', and through the similarly biblical word
'plagues'. Plagues also suggests disease and especially the deadly Black
Plague. Hence Blake evokes the image of God's punishment of sin. As the
image of the charming plague doctor at the start of this essay suggests, it's

like something out of *Night of the Living Dead*. Corruption so potent can, indeed, even transform a celebration of new life into an image of death, as in the startling oxymoron of the 'marriage hearse'.

## Songs of Innocence and Experience

*London* is from *Songs of Experience* (1792), the companion piece to his earlier *Songs of Innocence*. Blake was an idealist who wanted to see a better, fairer world. The front covers signal the different tones of the two books; where the Innocence image is maternal and comforting, the Experience images is sombre and suggests mourning for a spiritual loss. In many of the Experience poems Blake analyses and criticizes the harsh values of his society. Throughout the collection, he protests against injustice and exploitation. He stands up as a champion of the poor and challenges the cruelty of those in power. In this enterprise,

Blake's spiritual guide was Christ who he called '<u>Jesus, the imagination</u>'.

Blake was an artist as well as a poet and his illustrations were an integral part of his poems. Many of the illustrations accompanying the *Innocence* poems are rich, boldly coloured, sensual designs, presenting children playing in harmonious relation within exuberantly fertile images of nature. In contrast the palette of the *Experience* is much narrower and gloomier, conjuring a shadow world, drained of colour, dominated by greys and blacks.

The characters in these images express suffering and misery. Boxed in by the borders of the page, they appear trapped in their oppressive worlds. It is interesting that Blake depicts himself as two figures in the illustration to *London*. He is both the angelic child guide and the old man lead through the circles of this particular depiction of hell. In other words, he is both innocence and experience. Significantly at the end of the poem the image of innocence has disappeared.

## An age of revolutions

Blake's *Songs of Innocence* poems generally focus on childhood and are celebratory and optimistic in tone; the 'Experience' poems are much angrier. This darkening of mood between the two may have been due to Blake's reaction to the French Revolution of 1789. Like other Romantic poets, initially Blake saw the revolution as a great uprising of the human spirit, a liberation of the masses from the corrupt and unjust powers of the State. But as time went on news filtered through to England of appalling massacres carried out by the revolutionary forces. Over time it was becoming apparent that the French Revolution would result in one form of tyranny, that of the Monarchy, being replaced by another, that of the Masses.

*London* crunched:

**WANDER – CHARTERED – MARK – WOE – EVERY – CRY – EVERY – MANACLES – CHIMNEY-SWEEPER – CHURCH – SOLDIER – PALACE – MIDNIGHT – HARLOT – NEW-BORN – HEARSE.**

# Rupert Brooke, *The Soldier*

## As swimmers into cleaness leaping

I first read Brooke's poem in an influential anthology of WWI poetry we were studying for A-level English, called *Up the Line to Death*. The anthology was arranged so that the poems conveyed a narrative of the war and mapped the changing attitudes to it as the war progressed. The first poems *Up the Line to Death* expressed great patrioitic excitement at the prospect of war. This fervour didn't, however, last long. Once the fighting had actually begun, the reality of prolonged trench warfare became horribly apparent and that initial bright enthusiasm seemed, with the benefit of hindsight, terribly naive, even foolish. In the light of the poems of Wilfred Owen, Siegfried Sassoon, Isaac Rosenberg and the other WWI poets it seemed dangerously misleading too. In fact, for anyone at all familiar with the conditions of trench warfare in WWI – the blasted landscapes, the infestations of lice and rats, the mud, the dead and dying stuck in no-man's-land, the relentless pounding of artillery, the terror of going 'over-the-top' – the description of this horror as 'cleaness', as Brooke had done, couldn't be more bitterly inappropriate. Brooke's five war sonnets were written before the war started and they suffer from the way brutal historical reality shattered their romantic idealism. It is, however, somewhat unfair to judge Brooke's poetry in this way. He could not have concieved of the reality of WWI and quite possibly, if he hadn't died near the start of the conflict, his poetry would have changed as the war dragged on.

## 'All that one could wish England's noblest sons to be'

Public school and Cambridge educated, athlete and poet, 'the handsomest young man in England', friends with the Bloomsbury Group[2], admired by Winston Churchill, Rupert Brooke [1887-1915] lived a short, but charmed life. A popular, charismatic figure with an infectious laugh, Brooke seems to have made friends quickly wherever he went. Among his friends were writers such as the novelists Henry James and Virginia Woolf and the poet W.B. Yeats. He also counted important politians, such as Churchill, as friends. A pin-up, golden boy for literature, after his early death from blood poisoning, Brooke came to be seen as the most poignant symbol for a lost generation of talented youth. He died abroad and he is buried on the Greek island of Scyros. So, as he predicted in this sonnet, a corner of a 'foreign field' does indeed contain his English bones.

## An English Heaven?

Think of England and Englishness and what comes to mind? Perhaps the Houses of Parliament, the Queen, Churchill, the works of William Shakespeare. Or orderly queuing, roast beef and Yorkshire pudding, warm beer, cricket, bingo. Probably how you think of England and the English depends on your own nationality. Possibly if you're Scottish or Irish or Welsh you might feel a little bit of hostility. Ditto if you're French. If you, or your, family are originally from one of the many former English colonies you may also have ambivalent feelings. The way in which you construct your sense of identity also comes into the equation. You might define yourself by your nationality, but equally you might see your gender, race, sexuality, religion, values and beliefs or the part of the country you come from as more significant in determining your sense of self. For Rupert Brooke, however, there was no ambivalence. In this idealist sonnet *The Soldier* Brooke defines himself entirely by his nationality; His Englishness is the most essential aspect of his self. And, like, many English people of his generation, and some people still today, Brooke thought of himself as superior to foreigners because he was lucky enough to be born in England and to be English.

---

[2] A group of writers, artists and thinkers famous for their aesthetic sensibilities and bohemian lifestyles.

One way to foreground the patriotism of Brooke's poem is to present it first to a class as a cloze exercise with the six references to England or English blanked out, along with the adjective 'foreign'. It could be interesting to see what words the pupils think could occupy those blanks.

Patriotism is the love of your country. Nationalism is a more extreme form of patriotism that involves feeling superior to other countries. Jingoism is nationalism expressed in aggressive, warlike foreign policies. While patriotism might be laudable, Nationalism and jingoism are potentially dangerous and divisive forces. And although it expresses noble, courageous, perhaps heroic sentiments, and even though these ideas are expressed eloquently in a graceful sonnet, the problem with Brooke's poem is that it's not just patriotic, it's nationalistic. For instance, Brooke writes that buried in the 'rich soil' of a 'foreign field' his corpse is made of 'richer dust'. Not only is English soil superior to foreign soil, but even English  dust is richer than foreign soil! Notice too how the metre subtly underscores the point, diminishing the foreign richness and emphasising the English [stressed syllables are in bold]:

'In **that** rich **earth** a **rich**er **dust** concealed'

In the sonnet's opening eight line, or what's technically called its octave, Brooke personifies England as a gentle mother figure, the motherland. Like a mother, England gave birth to the poet, 'bore' him and like a mother it nurtured him into the man he became. Moreover, England is also presented as being like God. Creating him from 'dust', 'shaping' him, England gives him consciousness, 'made [him] aware'. Like a loving mother or loving God, England also cleanses and blesses him with its rivers and sunshine.

Clearly, the poem expresses a sentimental and idealised image of England and, indeed, of the soldier. Brooke was a key member of a group of poets called the Georgians who were popular in the early years of the twentieth century. Heavily influenced by Wordsworth, Georgian poetry is characterised by its 'idealistic preoccupation with rural youthful motifs'[3]. Characteristically Georgian poetry employed traditional poetic forms and its chief subject was nature. There is a gentle, romantic innocence to Georgian poetry and its style and after WWI its concerns suddenly seemed old-fashioned, out-moded and inadequate for expressing the new machine age. The avant-garde experimentalism and fashion for fragmentation in Modernism can be understood as a rejection of the aesthetics and themes of Georgian poetry.

Brooke's vision of England is of a timeless rural idyll: The poem includes 'rivers', 'flowers', 'suns' and 'English air' and it is a place of freedom where the poet can 'roam'. There's no mention of English cities, or English slums, or motor cars or any trace or taint at all of the modern world. Nor, in a poem about a soldier is there any sense of conflict or warfare. And, of course, Brooke's poem is a sonnet, a form most characteristically associated with love poetry. It's an appropriate choice of form for a poet expressing such perfect love for their country.

---

[3] https://www.poetryfoundation.org/poems-and-poets/poets/detail/rupert-brooke

## Hearts at peace and the old lie

Known as a 'volta', traditionally in a sonnet there is a turn in the ninth line, i.e. the first line of the last six. The volta marks a shift in perspective; if the octave asks a question, the sestet [last six lines] offers an answer. In Brooke's poem, however, the sestet develops a further amplification of the ideas expressed in the octave. Instead of there being a tension, or debate, or even conflict in the poem, in *The Solder* there is only harmony. The form of the poem expresses and embodies harmonious relations, like those between man and country. A steady, unruffled iambic pentameter also keeps the lines ticking along easily and Brooke uses full rhymes so that each rhyme chimes perfectly with its partner.

Brooke offers the comforting idea that the heroic self-sacrifice he makes will lead to the soldier becoming purified, 'all evil shed away', to become part of God, 'a pulse in the eternal mind'. And even in death, he will be able to return the generous favours England has bestowed upon him. Of course, in some ways this poem enacts this promise; every time someone reads its celebration of England, Brooke is giving back a little of what he was given. Once again, the vision is idealised as the poet focuses only on positive life experiences – dreams, laughter, friendship, gentleness, peace. His is a strikingly unaggressive and unwarlike soldier. As we will see when we read Owen's *Dulce et Decorum Est*, the true experience of war wasn't anything like Brooke's dreamy romantic imaginings. Though they were not addressed to Brooke specifically, Owen's lines at the end of his poem refute the sentiments expressed in Brooke's sonnets. Owen address a 'friend' who has been telling 'children' with 'high zest' what he calls bluntly 'the old lie' that it could be sweet and glorious to lay down your life for your country.

*The Soldier* crunched:

**DIE – FOREIGN – FOREVER – RICHER – ENGLAND – LOVE – ENGLISH – BLEST – HEART – ETERNAL – BACK – HAPPY – GENTLENESS - PEACE**

# Lord Byron, *She Walks in Beauty*

Lord Byron, or George Gordon Byron, is a love poet with a notorious reputation. Famously labelled 'mad, bad and dangerous to know', Byron was renowned for his flamboyance, condemned for his immoral lifestyle and chased for his huge debts. Following rumours of incest with his half-sister, he fled England, exiling himself in Europe and he died of a fever in Greece aged 36. During his life he was one of the second generation of Romantic poets, which included Percy Bysshe Shelley and John Keats.

This poem is famous for its rich lyricism compressed into such a short work. Byron's most famous other poems, such as *Don Juan* are epically long, but here we find complex language and imagery distilled into a pithy snapshot of a strange, dreamlike, entrancing female. Like Keats's *La Belle Dame,* it's not really a love poem; it's more of an infatuation or obsession poem. The fascination with which this woman is described is remarkably similar to those descriptions of nature's beauty which so captivated Romantic poets. More particularly, the Romantic poets' idea of nature is that it can sometimes lure you in with chilling and otherworldly power, just like the woman does in ***She walks in Beauty***. She's made into a 'type' by the vision of the poem's enraptured speaker, a generic desirable goal made more of an achievement through presenting her as distant, unattainable, mysterious.

## Superficiality

Whilst it's true to say that the poem has lots of superficial elements, it's also true that it makes the most of these. Superficiality shines through the language. The curiously generic description of the woman is made delicate and one-dimensional by the fact that the speaker refuses to talk of anything else. The perfect metre of the opening lines, in particular, signals a surface-level perfection that can be delicately wobbled or disrupted, like the glassy surface of a pond in the wind- 'she <u>walks</u> in <u>beauty, like</u> the <u>night</u>/ of <u>cloudless climes</u> and <u>starry skies</u>'.

'Pure', 'cloudless', 'tender', 'sweet', 'at peace', 'innocent', this is a woman that does nothing but smile and be a vessel for grace and physical attractiveness- her only facial expressions are rather blank [like 'thoughts serenely sweet express'] and the time when her face appears at all engaged is where she has 'smiles that win' to remember 'days in goodness spent'. Those in the 19th century just as much as those in the 21st century knew perfectly well that a paragon such as this did not exist- Byron is painting with the literary brushes of sensuousness and physical experience to create the feelings of awe and perhaps real reverence for an idealised object, not a real woman.

Byron deliberately doesn't create a complex and multifaceted character, nor does he provide a snapshot of a heroine from one of his epic poems. This is a different exercise- he capitalises on the short structure he is using to paint a static image, suspended in time. An admirer of the Augustan poets Pope and Dryden, characteristically in this poetry Byron was a satirist. He could be withering, for instance, about his fellow Romantic Poets; habitually he referred to the Lake poets, Wordsworth and Coleridge, as the 'pond poets' and rather rudely renamed the former Turdsworth. <u>Is there any part of this poem that comes across as satirical to you?</u>

## Keep your distance?

Byron was a widely-travelled man, especially with regard to the Far East; it is easy to see the sensory impact of rich and foreign lands on his work. Nowadays the description 'oriental' isn't really used, because the root of the word suggests that the east revolves round the West [and we know perfectly well that the West isn't the centre of the universe!] However, Byron uses language that would have typically conjured up images of the exotic, of the foreign, of the 'other', in a world where trading passages made exposure to the Far East increasingly easy, and where the East was seen as a world of danger, intrigue and dark magic.

The woman described in the poem is described as the 'night'. This is curious as the night is something that co-exists with day, but never coincides with it, shrouded by mystery and revolving as the dark face of the Earth- always chasing the sun. Byron talks about her delicate, ideal balance by describing 'one shade the more, one ray the less'- like the encroaching of night upon day. Like a pair of compasses, the woman occupies the place of night; removed, and slightly out of reach, yet always faithfully revolving around the light. Perhaps the speaker of the poem takes the place of the figure always separated from this mysterious woman, but always part of her presence; this would give the impression that the woman is removed and unattainable, and we know how much male love poets like talking about women who are aloof and unattainable!

Another interesting aspect of the woman's appearance is the emphasis on her darkness and her mystique. She is at once 'all that's best of dark and bright', at once being two things- seductive because of her glittering 'smiles that win, the tints that glow' but cloaked in 'shade' that makes her all the more alluring. Her 'raven tress' and the 'starry skies' indicate that impact of Orientalism on Byron's work- the attraction to something that is exotic and strange, and the fetishisation of other cultures because they seem so far away from our own. Women from other countries, especially Asia, were frequently fetishized in this way to create the narrative of their unattainability and therefore heighten the difficulty [and hence reward] of the 'conquest'.

For an example of how the Romantic poets in particular used Orientalism to aestheticise those from eastern countries, have a look at *Kubla Khan* by Coleridge. The paradise there, 'where blossomed many an incense-bearing tree', creates that same kind of still, perfect world that Byron's 'mysterious girl' inhabits. She seems to radiate from with, 'softly lighten[ed] o'er her face', 'the tints that glow', 'mellowed to that tender light'.

Do you think the speaker is interested in speaking to this woman or is he happy to have her kept at a distance? Why?

## Light and darkness

It's an interesting study of subjectivity that this woman can only be seen in the context of light, and is completely defined by how she is shaded- 'one shade the more, one ray the less'. The night that she is compared to is itself defined by 'starry skies'. She is made purely aesthetic, purely a physical being, by the fact that she can only be seen in light and has no obvious internal worth or complexity. Ironically, though she does not speak, her body speaks for her. Her cheeks or brow, in particular are described, somewhat improbably as 'eloquent', although the adjective could also be read as describing her smiles. Apparently her mind is also at peace [so basically there's nothing going on in her head] and her heart's 'love is innocent' [so she's never experienced any kind of relationship].

Alternatively, though she is defined by light, she can also be seen by it even when it is dark, like a beacon in 'the night / of cloudless climes'. She seems to have an inner radiance, generating her own light and this draws men to her, like a beacon. Or perhaps like moths to a flame. The fact that she remains removed throughout the poem suggests her inner light is like a lighthouse, warning ships away from a rocky shore. Is it possible that beneath the apparent serene beauty of this woman, hidden under the elegant and smooth poetic metre, and tucked inside the seemingly flattering imagery lurks something darker, dangerous and more threatening? The idea that a woman's beauty is dangerous is, of course, a common thread running through literature, but especially so at the time of the Romantic Movement. As Keats's *La Belle Dame Sans Merci* illustrates the vampire genre really took root by making female sexuality demonic and otherworldly. Can Byron's lady be read in the same way as some sort of femme fatale? Is the poem the dreamy expression of a bewitched potential victim?

This woman isn't blonde and beautiful, like an innocent child or angel. Rather she is dark [which brings into play the obvious negative connotations of 'darkness'] and 'of the night', a meaning which would have had much more impact on Byron's contemporary audience [particularly given his own liaisons with sex workers and other sexual encounters that would have been deemed immoral or illegal at the time]. Her hair is described as 'raven' black and ravens are, of course, associated with death and evil. Perhaps her description also implies innate sexual knowledge, her 'winning' smile luring the speaker [and the reader in] to her trust and affection.

In the end, though, this reading feels like forcing the poem into something it isn't. The significance of the various references to darkness in the poem is not due to connotations of evil or death, but rather that the lady is an ideal because in her the opposites of dark and light are perfectly reconciled. Yes, the poet is entranced by this figure and she does remain remote and rather ethereal. But there's nothing really convincing to suggest that her beauty and goodness is a trap luring in the besotted male.

What is certain in this poem is that the speaker uses the technique of synecdoche [using a part of something to describe the whole]. The only physical things we learn about the woman is a lot about her eyes, her face, and her dark hair, but the rest of her is presumably shrouded in the same darkness as the night which imposes as shade to make 'one ray the less'.

**She Walks in Beauty** crunched:

WALKS – BEAUTY – NIGHT – STARRY – DARK – BRIGHT – EYES – TENDER – HEAVEN – SHADE – RAY – GRACE – RAVEN – LIGHTENS – SERENELY – PURE – DEAR – ELOQUENT – SMILES – GOODNESS – PEACE – LOVE – INNOCENT

# Imtiaz Dharker, *Living Space*

Born in Lahore and brought up in Glasgow, poet, artist and documentary film-maker, Imtiaz Dharker describes herself as a 'Scottish Muslim Calvinist' adopted by India and married into Wales. Dharker's art work can be seen on her website: http://www.imtiazdharker.com.

 If I were teaching this poem, I would present it to a class first in prose form. You could ask a class what sort of text this might be and then ask them to identify the 'poetic' qualities. Finally ask them to set it out on the page as a poem. Explore what effects, if any, different arrangements of the words can have.

'There are just not enough straight lines. That is the problem. Nothing is flat or parallel. Beams balance crookedly on supports thrust off the vertical. Nails clutch at open seams. The whole structure leans dangerously towards the miraculous. Into this rough frame, someone has squeezed a living space. And even dared to place these eggs in a wire basket, fragile curves of white hung out over the dark edge of a slanted universe, gathering the light into themselves, as if they were the bright, thin walls of faith.'

## Higgledy-piggledy architecture

Presented like this is it obvious that the text is a poem? Probably not. There's no rhyme scheme, or metre, very few recognisable poetic devices, such as alliteration or metaphor. 'Clutch' is used metaphorically and the 'egg' is a symbol compared to 'faith', which has 'walls'. But much of the rest of the language is very straightforward. Language doesn't come much more straightforward, for instance, than 'that is the problem'. The style is conversational, as if we have joined the middle of a discussion. At first the subject isn't clear. What doesn't have enough 'straight lines'? Does the poet mean that there need to be more 'straight lines' in the world or in life? Is this something to do with promoting directness, rather than, say, crookedness? It is only later in the poem, once we have heard about 'beams' and 'nails' and 'the whole structure' with someone living inside it that we realise the poem is about a building someone has managed to turn into a home. Perhaps that withholding of information could be seen as poetic.

## The whole structure leans dangerously

What is gained by the poet's arrangement of the words into verse form? It seems that the poem is constructed almost randomly without any underlying structure or frame. As well as having no metre or rhyme scheme, there appears to be no principle underpinning the length of lines. The shortest lines are just three words long, or four syllables, and the longest are six words or eight syllables. The effect of the inconsistent line lengths is that the poem looks untidy on the page, with some stunted lines and others sticking out awkwardly from the rest. On top of that, sentences are broken seemingly randomly across lines, such as, 'That / is the problem', 'flat / or parallel' and 'Beams / balance'. In the second and fourth lines caesuras break the line in two. Mostly the sentences are short and stubby, though the last sentence, beginning 'Into this rough frame' stretches over the stanza break and runs for a total of 11 lines to the last full stop of the poem. Rhymes pop up from time to time - 'that'/ 'flat'; 'beams'/ 'seams'; 'space'/ 'place'/ 'faith' - but there doesn't seem to be any organised pattern or coherent scheme. There is a noticeable

65

lack of conjunctions to connect sentences and lines together. There's not even a single conjunction in the first stanza and the only one in the whole poem ['and'] bolts the two stanzas only very loosely together. And these two stanzas are also of different shapes and unbalanced lengths.

This seems like a catalogue of dire construction failures:

1. No rhyme scheme or metre = lack of stable substructure
2. Random line length, awkwardly varied
3. Random breaking of lines, or overstretching of them
4. Random rhyming
5. Lack of conjunctions to connect the parts of the poem together
6. Ugly design fault in relationship between the two stanzas.

If the poem were a building and I were a building inspector, you might assume that it would be condemned and demolition promptly ordered. It is tempting.

But, before we order the bulldozers to move in, look at the poem on the page, consider its irregularities and loose, apparently ramshackle construction and you'll realise its form mimics the slum building its describing. Both poem and building are haphazard looking structures leaning 'dangerously', decks of cards that are on the verge of collapse. Because, not only are the constituent parts of each edifice loosely constructed, they are, therefore, under strain. In the case of the house, this is indeed dangerous. The beams, for instance, balance 'crookedly' as if they might buckle [this adverb may also suggest criminal negligence in the constructing of the house]. Dharker also employs a violent verb 'thrust' to convey the pressure on the supports. The fact that the building 'leans' is itself a little alarming. But probably the most disturbing detail is the description of the nails which 'clutch at open seams'.

First off, the verb 'clutch' signals desperation. Secondly, that small preposition, 'at' adds to the alarm as this suggests whatever the nails are trying to reach is too far away. If you 'clutch at' something you can easily miss. The adjective 'open' could obviously suggest gaps, presumably unintentional ones, which in turn confirms that the nails are not up to their task. Lastly 'seams' is more usually applied to clothing. In this context it implies the flimsiness of the material. Seams are also the bits where things are supposed to come together; they hold the whole structure in place. The phrase 'fall apart at the seams' might spring uneasily to mind of our imaginary building inspector.

## Over the dark edge

The precariousness of the building is also conveyed through calling it 'miraculous', as in it's a miracle it doesn't collapse. This adjective has another function, however, paving the way for the introduction of 'faith' at the end of the poem. Another miracle is that someone has managed to turn this building into a home, a 'living space', in both senses of that phrase. Moreover, they've 'dared' to hang out a basket of eggs. The eggs have several things in common with the building; both are 'fragile', their shapes are curved and both  seem to be defying probability in remaining whole and unbroken. The eggs are in an even more precarious state; small, delicate objects, they are hanging 'out' over the ominously 'dark edge' of a huge space, a 'universe' that is itself dangerously out of kilter, 'slanted'. Despite this, the eggs mysteriously draw 'light / into themselves'. Like the houses, eggs are also living spaces, they contain life within their shells. Moreover, they are living spaces from which new life in the future can be born. Dharker suggests that they are also like faith which itself, like a building, is described as having 'walls'. So, the building is like the egg which is like faith which is like a building. In a 'slanted', precarious universe, with dark edges, these fragile structures all manage, miraculously, against the odds, to sustain life and provide us with hope for the future. And I expect the poet might hope for the same of her rickety-looking but actually cleverly constructed poem.

*Living Space* collapsed:

**STRAIGHT - PROBLEM - FLAT - CROOKEDLY - THRUST - CLUTCH - DANGEROUSLY - MIRACULOUS - ROUGH - SOMEONE - LIVING - AND - EGGS - FRAGILE - DARK - UNIVERSE - LIGHT - INTO - FAITH**

# Emily Dickinson, *As Imperceptibly as Grief*

## Space oddity

During her lifetime [1830-1886] only about ten of Emily Dickinson's poems were published. However, after the poet's death, her sister discovered a box containing numerous volumes full of poems. Over time, nearly two thousand poems, which had been carefully hand stitched into little books, began to be published. And slowly Dickinson's reputation grew and grew. So much so that nowadays this famously reclusive poet is considered one of America's greatest poets and a feminist literary icon.

Like her first readers, it's likely that the first thing that strikes any student reading a Dickinson poem for the first time is its oddity, its intensity and unconventionality. Certainly, that's what struck her contemporaries, who tried to straighten out and tidy up Dickinson's poems, giving them titles, punctuating them more conventionally and squeezing their typically gaunt forms into more regular shapes. Only over time did readers come to realise that her artistic genius lay exactly in her unconventionality and that idiosyncrasies, such as her affection for hyphens, were fundamental aspects of this originality.

*As Imperceptibly as Grief* may feature six hyphens and only one full stop, but in this poem the dashes come in the same places, i.e. the ends of lines. They are also of the same size. In some poems, Dickinson used vertical hyphens and ones of various sizes. Placed at the ends of lines, in this poem her hyphens form a sort of opened-ended link; on one side is a word - on the other the white space of the rest of the page. Or, perhaps, we should think of this as a link to the infinite. The other obvious oddity in Dickinson's poems is her use of capitalisation. This seems almost antiquated, harking back to a time when nouns were routinely capitalised in written English. In this poem it is, indeed, nouns, both abstract and concrete, that are capitalised, but so too is one adjective, 'Beautiful'. The reader's eye is naturally drawn to these capitalised words, 'like weeds growing between pavement slabs' as one critic puts it. A list of the capitalised words effectively crunches the poem:

GRIEF – SUMMER – PERFIDY – QUIETNESS – TWILIGHT – NATURE – AFTERNOON – DUSK – MORNING – GRACE – GUEST – WING – KEEL.

The list highlights the confusing progress of time in the poem, from twilight to afternoon to dusk to morning. Either time is moving in jumps and starts or we're moving forwards and then backwards in time. That might, however, not be the first oddity that leaps out at the puzzled reader. To me, the word 'perfidy' sticks out because it's such an uncommon, literary word and because it means betrayal or deceit or disloyalty. Those meanings appear incongruous and disproportionate in a poem about the natural and inevitable passing of summer into autumn.

There are a few other unusual words that might trip us up at first. 'Sequestered', for example, means hide away and 'harrowing' means acutely distressing. But it's the odd combination of words, the peculiar, intense phrasing that's most striking and disorientating at first. Consider, for example, the references in quick succession to a 'wing', a 'keel' and to summer as a female recluse, slipping away at the end of the poem. It takes a little decoding to work out that the first two are imagined as things the latter is without. So, summer is first like a bird, but without wings, then a line latter it is like a boat without a keel and finally it is a woman eager to leave. Strictly speaking this is what's known as mixed metaphor – if summer is like a bird it cannot have a keel. Yet, the swift elusive, shapeshifting quality of what is already itself an abstract and hence difficult to imagine concept, summer, fits the idea of it slipping away into something equally intangible and difficult to define, 'the beautiful'. The description of the summer is like the whole poem – we can understand all the words, but somehow the meaning is uncertain, mysterious and seems to slip through our attempts to define it.

Take another example, the use of similes in the poem and more precisely the similes within similes, like a set of Russian dolls. The opening two lines propose a similarity between the process of grief and the movement from summer to autumn. So, concept 'a' [grief] is like concept 'b' [summer]. In the next lines we are told that the shared qualities of 'a' and 'b' are not quite like 'c' [perfidy]. In the succeeding lines another new idea is introduced, 'd' [Quietness], which seems to be an aspect of the shared quality of 'a' and 'b' – its 'imperceptibility'. This 'd' shares qualities with 'e' [twilight] and/or 'f' [nature]. We have then a run of three more abstract nouns, 'dusk', 'morning' and 'grace', which we'll label 'g', which are like 'h', a guest, who is keen to depart. As the repetition of the comparative word 'as' makes clear, we then have another swift run of connections of things that are like each other: So, to summarise and make things crystal clear: 'a' is like 'b' which is not quite like 'c', but a quality of 'a' and 'b', 'd' is like 'e' and/or 'f' which is also 'g' which is like 'h'. If we were clever enough we might be able to represent this mesh of complex inter-relationships in a neat mathematical equation. But unfortunately, we're not that clever. Anyhow, the point is that it's no wonder Dickinson's original readers found her work eccentric and rather

brain-draining. And that teachers and students continue to find her it challenging.

Because, if that were not enough, there's even more obscurity. Dickinson distils and intensifies language by cutting out function words. But these little words serve a function in language; they can help us, for instance, to understand how more important words and phrases connect to each other. Consider the following lines:

'The Morning foreign shone–
A courteous, yet harrowing Grace'

The absence of 'with' at the end of the first of these lines means we can read the second in three different ways. Either the morning shone with a strange grace, or the fact that the morning was shining was itself a strange grace, or the fact that the morning's shining was 'foreign' was a strange grace.

Add to that the poem's lack or rhyme and a metre that sets off regularly enough, alternating, like a ballad, between four stress and three stressed lines, but soon goes wildly off the rails, and we might be beginning to sympathise with those first readers and their desire to regularise Dickinson's poems.

Despite the obscurities and ambiguities can we make sense of Dickinson's poem? Well we'll certainly have a go.

### Tell the truth, but tell it slant

Dickinson's poem expresses the inevitability of the loss of precious things, things that slip away from us almost unnoticed and the effect this loss has on us. Though Dickinson seems to be writing about summer, if we bear in mind the fact that her style is characteristically indirect and elliptical, we can surmise that the summer is standing in symbolically for another loss, or that the loss of summer provides the poet with a comforting way of rationalising another more personal loss that lies semi-hidden, half-buried behind this poem. Dickinson scholars are not certain about this, but the consensus suggests that when she was in her twenties the poet fell in love, probably with an older, married preacher called Charles Wadsworth. Though she shared some precious time with Wadsworth, it seems her love was not requited, Wadsworth moved far away and Dickinson became a recluse, hardly seeing any visitors. So the story goes. The loss of summer is compared by Dickinson to 'grief' and other words and phrases in the poem hint at the painful break-up of a relationship: As we've already said, 'perfidy' seems an excessive word to use in the overt context of a poem about summer; so too does 'harrowing', meaning acute distress. But these are definitely words someone who feels betrayed and heartbroken might use.

The idea in the second stanza of 'quietness' growing more profound suggests a greater awareness of absence, the sense of great emptiness and aloneness. Once the thing/person who has brought sunshine has left, the poet's life dims to become a protracted half-light half-life, a long 'twilight'. Surely the reference to 'nature' spending time alone, 'sequestered', is a displaced image of the reclusive poet hiding from the outside world. Similar ideas run through the third stanza. There is a sense of stasis in the reference to dusk, another word for twilight. It 'drew earlier in' because of the loss of light. Conventionally references to morning, particularly in the Romantic tradition out of which Dickinson's poetry emerged, signify new hope, new beginnings. Now it seems alien, 'foreign', as if everything has grown unfamiliar in the new landscape of loss. The image of the guest, keen to be gone, doesn't need much decoding, but why is their presence, and specifically their 'grace', 'courteous but harrowing'? Perhaps the courteousness prolongs the leave-taking of the guest and that prolongation is an agony for the poet because she knows it must end with permanent separation. Perhaps courteousness is agonising, because polite relationships are no substiture for love.

And suddenly, in the last stanza, despite their lack of the means of motion, the summer/ lover is gone. The reference to 'our summer' might make us think of the summer as their happiness together. Read this way, the poem is an elliptical take on the central shaping incident of Dickinson's adult life. Despite the grief, the poem ends with a consoling image of the summer/ lover / their relationship escaping from the poet's restricted and often oppressive existence 'into the beautiful'. There's an admirable stoic backbone in Dickinson's poem that allows her cope with grief and allow it slip away, almost unnoticed. The summer may have been short, but summers return each year, and this summer gave her this extraordinary poem.

*As Impeccably as Grief* crushed:

**GRIEF – AWAY – IMPERCEPTIBLE – PERFIDY – QUIETNESS – TWILIGHT – HERSELF – SEQUESTERED – DUSK – FOREIGN – HARROWING – GUEST – WING – KEEL – ESCAPE – BEAUTIFUL**

# Rita Dove, *Cozy Apologia*

Currently the Commonwealth Professor of English at the University of Virginia, Rita Dove is a distinguished American poet and critic. Dove was the youngest ever American poet laureate and the first ever African American to hold this position; she was also only the second African American to receive the Pulitzer Prize for Poetry.

## Lovey dovey

An 'apologia' is a written defence or explanation of one's motives. Hence the title of Dove's poem immediately makes the reader curious about what she's going to apologise for and why she feels she needs to do this. In its combination of a familiar, ordinary and tactile adjective 'cozy' with a more, erudite, Latinate and abstract noun, the title also encapsulates Dove's poetic mode. What does she feel impelled to apologise for? It seems that she's apologising for being 'happy' and comfortable in a relationship. Rather than producing poetry of extremes and the 'Divine', she writes instead a poem about the cosiness of 'the ordinary'. The only extreme, the 'hurricane', in this poem is kept firmly outside and only accentuates the couple's mutual security inside their home. Clearly there's a danger here that such cosiness might appear twee, a little complacent or even smug. Dove avoids that with touches of humour and a brief indication of quite different, darker emotions.

The poet addresses her beloved in a conversational idiom and tells him she could make him her muse, implying that all her thoughts return to him: 'I could pick up anything and think of you'. A number of ordinary things in her immediate vicinity come to mind as prompts, but swiftly she moves beyond these to imagine him as a 'hero'. Specifically, he is like a gallant knight of old, 'astride a dappled mare', fully furnished with 'silver stirrups' and 'chain mail'. And what is more, he's riding to rescue her, to set her free from some imagined imprisonment or peril, and to win her affections, shooting 'arrows to the heart'. Like a medieval James Bond, simultaneously he gives her the eye while keeping the other 'firm upon the enemy'. A nice trick if you can do it, and

ride a horse, at the same time firing off love arrows. Clearly this isn't an entirely serious image. The gentle comic tone is further indicated by references to his legs braced 'as far apart / as standing in silver stirrups will allow' and to the sort of exaggerated gestures associated with amateur dramatics, 'with furrowed brow' and 'one eye smiling'. Though, when you think about it, the latter might be rather hard to convey.

The form of the poem is another signal of the comic nature of the poem. Scan a few lines and you'll work out their written in quite bouncy iambic pentameters [stressed beats are in bold]:

'I **could** pick **an** y **thing** and **think** of **you** -
This **lamp**, the **wind** -still **rain**, the **gloss** y **blue**'

The metrical bounciness is enhanced by the couplet rhyme scheme and the use of full, masculine rhymes. Each pair of lines ends with a satisfying sonic resolution as the rhyme clicks neatly in place. Iambic pentameters in couplet form are also called 'heroic couplets' and this form is especially associated with writers such as Geoffrey Chaucer and Alexander Pope. In their work the heroic couplet is often used for satirical and comic effect. Hence Dove's poem begins within this tradition of comic writing. Dove's language may be down-to-earth and conversational, but the poem's form is highly literary.

## Cussing up a storm

There's quite a switch in the second stanza from the world of chivalry and Romances to the modern [though already dated] technology of 'compact discs' and 'faxes'. The thought of 'risks' prompts the poet to think of the 'hurricane' that is making its way up the coast. This force of nature doesn't just potentially disturb the outside landscape, it also disturbs the inner one of the poet's mind, bringing old memories back to the surface of perception. Though the language of the poem remains settled and the tone calm, there is some sense of discombobulation in the form: Like fissures, caesuras start appearing and the orderly couplet rhyme scheme is disrupted - 'reminiscences' does not find a pair in 'boys', and even when it does reach its delayed pair, this is only the slightest of rhymes, 'senseless' - 'boys' must wait for three further lines before it's matched with 'Floyd's'.

The disturbance stirs up 'awkward' memories of old romances. Through their various inadequacies these only serve, however, to emphasise the implied qualities of the poem's addressee. The boys are 'worthless', 'hollow' and effeminate - they all had 'sissy names' - and their talents are very much in the singular. At this point, Dove introduces a mixture of sensory and figurative imagery, describing the boys as 'thin as liquorice and as chewy'. You don't need to be an ardent feminist to know that often in the past women have been compared to food by men, just one among many ways women have been presented as objects for male gratification. Dove's reversal of this norm is underlined using a word that many women find demeaning if applied to them, the adjective 'sweet'. This is another way in which these boys are diminished, emasculated in contrast to the Big Bad wolf of storm Floyd and that traditional symbol of gallant masculine virility, the knight.

Hurricane Floyd may be 'cussing up a storm', but the poet and her partner seem pretty safe from its reach. This last stanza is all about what these two share. He lives in an 'aerie', figuratively suggesting he's like a bird, a majestic

77

eagle, and she's 'perched' in her version of the same. The furnishing also match each other's, 'twin desks, computers, hardwood floors'. The singular pronoun widens into a comfortable and comforting 'we' and 'us'. And here we come to the self-conscious apology for this wholesome cosiness and dull everydayness: 'it's embarrassing, this happiness'; 'good for us'; 'when has the ordinary ever been news?' The rhetorical questions anticipate potential objections, such as that the poet has settled for comfortableness in their life and as the subject for her poetry when they should be reaching for true inspiration, capitalised as the 'Divine'. Readers weaned on the violent emotional turbulences of American confessional poetry or on more politically engaged work by black writers, might find this style and subject a little tame and unchallenging, perhaps. Dove's poem is colour-neutral and her language is polite Standard English. Aren't poets supposed to be mad, bad and dangerous to know? [see Byron, L.] Just when the poem is in danger of settling into overly comfy mode the mention of 'melancholy' adds a bit of emotional depth. And this gives the shorter, punchier final line a bit more heft.

The three solid looking, substantial stanzas of the poem suggest the rock-solidity of the relationship. The first stanza is written in heroic couplets, but this pattern is disrupted once the hurricane's impact is felt. The pattern develops into cross rhyme in the final stanza with a couplet in the middle lines, 'happiness'/ 'good for us'. Though this is a different pattern to how the poem began, it's a suitably harmonious one, in which the pattern of the first five lines is matched by that in the second five.

*Cozy Apologia* crunched:
[As this is a fairly long poem, I'm going to apply a little more pressure to the crunch]

**YOU - HERO - HEART - FREE - HURRICANE - REMINISCENCES - SWEET - AERIE - TWIN - CONTENT - GOOD - ORDINARY - NOTHING - BLUES - YOU**

# Carol Ann Duffy, *Valentine*

### Tell me the truth about love

Right from the very first word, the negative 'no' in her first abrupt, truncated sentence Duffy makes it clear hers isn't going to be any kind of conventional love poem. This poet is not going to employ conventional symbols of love, nor offer these tired, old objects as her Valentine's gift: 'Not a red rose or a satin heart'. The first symbol was most famously used by Robert Burns in his lovely love poem *Oh my love's like a red, red rose*. Within the first four words of Duffy's she has dismissed this symbol and all it connotes about the nature of love. Instead she's going to give her beloved an 'onion'. And Duffy might be the first poet or person who's ever lived who thinks that love is like an object Wikipedia defines as a 'swollen edible bulb used as a vegetable'. Certainly, an onion seems an unlikely symbol for love and Duffy sticks full stops at the end of each of the first two lines to emphasise the comic surprise of this object. Certainly, it would be hard not to be a tad disappointed by this inexpensive and distinctly unromantic gift if you were the 'you' in the poem. What would be a less romantic gift? A pair of socks? A saucepan? A revision book, perhaps on poetry? An onion has got to be right up there with the world's worst possible valentine gifts.

In the rest of the poem, Duffy develops the comparison between a loving relationship and an onion. This sort of extended metaphor is technically known as a conceit. A famous example runs through Shakespeare's sonnet 18, whose title *Shall I compare thee to a Summer's day* rather gives away the nature of the conceit. Conceits are particularly associated with Renaissance writers and especially with a group of poets now known rather grandly as The Metaphysicals. Typically, Metaphysical poets used conceits to demonstrate their poetic wit; the more unlikely the things being compared, the greater the wit required to show how they are actually rather alike. The leading Metaphysical poet, John Donne, for instance, in a move even less romantic than Duffy's onion compared love to a flea. Yes, a flea. And he employed it in order to try to seduce his beloved! Yes, a flea. And that highlights another way in which  Duffy boldly defies convention. She employs a device, a conceit, used extensively by male poets and used by those male poets to seduce female subjects. In Duffy's poem, however, the conceit is not used rhetorically to seduce. Instead it serves as a corrective to clichéd, soppy, sentimental ideas of love; her onion offers a stiff dose of pungent realism. As she says, though it might be less romantic, and though perhaps her partner expresses some reluctance accepting the message, Duffy has taken off the rose-tinted spectacles of Valentine's Day, and is 'trying to be truthful', about their relationship and about all relationships. And about the true nature of love.

So Duffy rejects conventional symbols, chooses an unconventional one and uses a conceit, but in an unconventional way. And the form of her poem is also unconventional. What's the most conventional form for a love poem? We've already mentioned it; of course, it's a limerick. I mean a sonnet, like Barrett Browning's. Duffy's poem is nothing like a sonnet, in fact it's nothing like any conventional closed or open form of poem because it's written in free verse and is highly irregular. This means that the lines and stanzas and rhythm and rhyme don't conform to any pre-set pattern; instead they follow their own unique, idiosyncratic impulses. This is another way in which Duffy implies her love and love itself is not regular, doesn't fit convention, is complex and difficult and unpredictable and, well, oniony.

Look at the poem on the page and seems rather slight and delicate, maybe even fragile. The lines move in a careful, perhaps even hesitant fashion. There are lots of stops and starts, full stops and short sentence fragments, such as 'take it' and 'lethal'. These help control the delivery of the poem and convey a sense of drama - a speaking voice, slowing down, pausing or growing more animated. The poem may look a little fragile and skeletal, however if so, it's a skeleton of steel.

## Love is like an onion

So, Ms. Duffy, tell us how exactly is love, or a relationship, like an onion? Well, it turns out they do have rather a lot of things in common. Firstly, the inside of an onion does look a bit like a moon, that eternal symbol of love in a relationship, and onion flesh is white, like light. And onions also have layers, which we can 'undress'. Not only that, but onions can make us cry through their sharp, intense aroma and thus, they can distort our perceptions. Moreover, the taste of an onion is so strong it lingers on the lips and in the mouth [try kissing someone who's just eaten cheese and onion crisps, or rather don't] and on one's fingers. After chopping an onion, a knife needs washing to get rid of the clingy scent. And lastly, its rings are platinum coloured and one ring could, if shrunk, serve as a very poor wedding-ring. So, despite seeming unlikely, an onion is shown to be an appropriate analogy for a relationship. Hats off to Duffy.

We might be persuaded by Duffy's wit. But it seems her addressee needs plenty of convincing. In the second line of the poem the poet passes over the gift. And she does so again four lines later in the opening word of the second stanza. After this there is a long pause. And then she explains again how she has not bought a clichéd present, this time round a 'cute-card or a kissogram' and again tries to give the beloved the 'onion'. Repetition of exactly the same line, 'I give you an onion' signals no progress has been made, despite the poet's tremendous efforts. We're back where we started. By the penultimate stanza, the gift still hasn't been accepted. Is there a touch or annoyance in the shift to the imperative? Again a very short line, just two simple monosyllables, finishes with an emphatic full stop and then a long blank line that suggests silence. As if the recipient is still considering whether to take it. Through such means Duffy helps us picture a little scene, a short piece of domestic drama, featuring repeated offer and repeated refusal. Certainly, the addressee needs a bit more of a nudge, because in the next line the poet makes a rather half-hearted seeming marriage proposal: 'a wedding-ring/ if you like'. That casual, 'if you like' makes it seem like an afterthought. Rather ominously straight afterward, as if the beloved has finally accepted the gift, comes the single word 'Lethal' and more portentous silence.

Why did the addressee need so much convincing? We said at the start that Duffy's poem tries to correct overly sickly and sentimental presentations of love and relationships; that the poem was a sharp taste of oniony realism. But the poet is also persuasive, just in a different way to those lusty Metaphysicals. The poet tries to persuade their lover about the true nature of their relationship. And it's not all sweetness and light. Take it, the poet says. If you dare.

*Valentine* crunched:

**ROSE – ONION – MOON – PROMISES – UNDRESSING – HERE – TEARS – LOVER – REFLECTION – GRIEF – TRUTHFUL – CUTE – ONION – FIERCE – POSSESSIVE – WE – LONG – TAKE – WEDDING-RING – IF – LETHAL – CLING - KNIFE**

We mentioned earlier that it'd be hard to imagine a less Romantic symbol of love or a worse Valentine's gift than an onion and suggested a few terrible alternatives. How about writing a version of *Valentine* replacing Duffy's onion with your own idea for the world's least romantic gift? We're so ashamed by our own version that we're going to hide it somewhere at the back of this book. But we're 100% confident you'll be able to produce something better...

My love for you is like diarrhea.... I just cant hold it in!

# Thomas Hardy, *A Wife in London*

## Everything can tell a story

As well as being a poet, Thomas Hardy [1840-1928] was, of course, a famous novelist. The narrative skills of the author of novels such as *Tess of the D'Urbervilles*, *Far from the Madding Crowd* and *Jude the Obscure* are evident in his Boer War poem *A Wife in London*. In quick novelistic strokes Hardy conjures the scene - the woman sitting alone in the 'tawny vapour', within the 'webby fold' on a City street feebly lit by the 'cold' and inconstant 'glimmer' of streetlamps. The adjective 'tawny' establishes the colour scheme - browny orange, while the more tactile 'webby fold on fold' suggests entrapment, like a fly. The woman sits 'in' the vapour as if isolated by it and as if it is an externalisation of her mood, perhaps. Hardy was fond of using pathetic fallacy, a device where the weather works as an analogue of a character's feelings, so that a rainy day = unhappiness and sunshine = a joyous mood and so forth. A common motif in Victorian and Gothic fiction, fog usually conveys perceptual uncertainty and obscurity. Hence it symbolises the fogginess of the woman's understanding of the tragedy that is to come. The simile of the candle, the 'waning taper', establishes the weakness of the light and the fact that its strength is lessening. As with the fog, a taper is a common symbol with the flame symbolising the human soul. Hence the image is ominous, implying that someone's death is coming. Perhaps even this woman's, sitting alone here in the half-light. As with their feeble illumination, the street-lamps also offer no heat, they 'glimmer cold', an image which implies a lack of comfort, perhaps even the indifference of the world around to the woman's sorry plight.

All this - character, scene, mood - is established in a concise first stanza, five short lines and just 28 words long in total. This would be impressive in any piece of writing, but in a Victorian poem this leanness and lack of verbal padding is especially striking. On the whole, Victorian literary style, like their taste in interior design, was for the rather heavily and richly upholstered. As any pupil who has read a Victorian novel will know, 'wordy' is a word that might spring unhappily to mind. Hardy's style here, in contrast, is a model of economy. His choice of metre adds to the sense of the story being sketched in quickly without any any excessive details. Hardy shifts between short three and four beat lines, trimeters and tetrameters, in his own variation on the story-telling ballad form.

In contrast to the muffled and static atmosphere of the first stanza, action immediately propels the second stanza forward. A dynamic verb and sound are used: The knock 'cracks smartly', quickly followed by another dynamic verb, this time visual, 'flashed'. Unnecessary parts of the narrative are skipped over - we don't need to know the knock was at the front door, nor do we see the woman rise and answer the door, nor hear any of the dialogue that could have followed. Hardy's style is more like a sketch than a detailed oil painting or perhaps a short film. Things move quickly. No sooner has the woman the letter in her hand than she has read it and is struggling to process its news. The fourth line is appropriately and bluntly cut short: 'Though shaped so shortly'. Just four words, only two beats form a momentary stay of execution before she, and we, discover that it is her husband who has died. The hyphens in the final line create small pauses and suggest the difficulty the wife has coming to terms with the dire information. Hence they draw us closer to her thoughts and feelings. Perhaps for a moment we imagine her hoping that the euphemistic 'fallen' doesn't, in fact, mean that he is dead. That his death happened in a vague other place, a 'South Land' that is 'far' away, adds further poignancy.

Of course, unlike the wife, we've known from the subtitle that a tragedy is coming. The dramatic irony makes the woman seem more helpless and deserving of our pity. But the subtitle also rather unsubtly guides us on how to read the man's death; it does not just evoke pathos, it is tragic. Similarly, Hardy forewarns of us before the second half of the poem that it will be ironic, in this case, bitterly ironic.

Sometimes Hardy has been thought of as a rather grimly pessimistic writer, prone to gloomy introspection. Undisputedly there is a pervasive fatalism in his work, a sense that try as hard as they might, the wills of puny individual humans can do nothing to halt or even deflect the great steamroller of destiny. Not only is the wider cosmic order often presented as indifferent to human suffering, like the 'cold' inanimate street-lamps, but it sometimes seems to be animated by an active malignancy, a desire to make Hardy's character suffer. At the end of *Tess of the D'Urbervilles*, for instance, Hardy writes about how the 'President of the Immortals' had finally finished his cruel 'sport' with her. The last two stanzas of *A Wife in London* could be cited as another case in point.

### His hand, whom the worm now knows

By a cruel irony, the husband's letter, with his jaunty plans for the future, arrives a day after news of his death. Now the fog has grown more oppressive, hanging 'thicker', a visual representation of the wife's deeper isolation. Again there is an absence of light; she reads his letter by the 'firelight flicker'. And this presumably is the morning, or at least early daytime as the postman has just come. Darkness, of courcse, carries its own symbolism. Perhaps, the darkness also indicates winter, a suitable month for this story. There is a horribly irony in how vigorously alive and packed with hope the letter seems to be. The handwriting is still 'fresh' and 'firm'. Presumably 'in highest feather' means something like in great spirits. The references to 'hand' suggest both the husband's writing, but also, for a ghostly moment, his physical body. Hence the image of the worm is a rather macabre one of his corpse being buried and turned to food. In a final turning of the tragic screw Hardy ends the poem with a poignant shift of tense. Up until this moment the action of the poem has been taking place in the present tense. What is the effect of this choice? What might be lost if the poem had been written in the past tense? As well as creating greater immediacy, the present tense seems to trap the wife in a permanent suspended state of the story simultaneously having happened and still be happening to her. The last line switches to the future tense and an agonising conditional 'they would learn'. That hopeful sounding 'would' was conditional on the husband surviving the Boer War.

## Woman much missed

Characters haunted by vivid memories of the past feature pervasively in Hardy's work. Often the haunted figure is Hardy himself, hearing, for instance, the ghost voice of his dead wife calling to him across a lonely landscape. The unnamed characters in this narrative poem are clearly representative, everyman figures. Their tragic experience, swiftly sketched in only around a hundred words or so, stands in for many other couples separated by war and, more specifically, women widowed and haunted by memories of a lost love. The protagonist is 'a', not 'the' wife. Hardy doesn't give us more specific details, such as what the woman looks like, or the interior of her house or, indeed, what class she comes from, in part because that would detract from this universality. He is more interested in character, mood, setting and the ironic structure of the narrative.

Normally comments on the form and structure of a poem focus on stanza patterns, rhyme schemes, and such like. And Hardy's use of cinquains with an unbalanced, ABBAB rhyme scheme contributes subtly to the unsettled feel of the poem. But more significant in this case is the narrative structure. This follows the recognisable convention of situation [woman in fog, first stanza] and then the inciting incident, complication or catalyst [messenger arrives, second stanza]. The next two stages of the narrative take place in a few lines - development and crisis happen at once [news of husband's death]. Instead of the final stages following, climax and resolution, the third stanza is a reprise of the first. This time Hardy arrests the narrative at the development stage, denying us the comfort of a resolution, leaving readers to imagine what might happen in the rest of the widow's life. In fact, the wife's perspective is almost entirely erased in the poem's second half. For instance, the letter's lines 'disclose' rather than 'she discovers' its contents. This absence makes the reader imagine the wife's feelings - it forces us to inhabit her perspective and fill in her possible thoughts. Again, characteristically and rather impressively for a Victorian male writer, Hardy is particularly interested in, and sympathetic to, the life experiences of women. In *Tess*, for instance, he attacked the hypocrisy of a society that could brand his protagonist a 'fallen woman' and ostracise her for having a child out of wedlock. And treat her like that, even though she was the victim of a possible rape and definitely of an abuse of power. Historically, I expect, the majority of war poems focus on the experience of soldiers and on battle. Hardy is less interested in that and more interested in the long-lasting after effects war, and other cruel fates, can have on the lives of ordinary people and, in particular, on the lives of women.

*A Wife in London* crushed:

**VAPOUR - CITY - WEBBY - WANING - COLD - CRACKS - FLASHED - DAZES - SHORTLY - FALLEN - THICKER - GOES - LETTER - FIRELIGHT - WORM - FRESH - RETURN - JAUNTS - SUMMER - LOVE**

# Seamus Heaney, *Death of a Naturalist*

## A strong gauze of sound

After the expectations set up by the rather melodramatic title, the content of Heaney's narrative lyric might appear at first to be disappointingly tame. Where we might ask is the promised/ threatened 'death'? We might feel this especially after reading the first long stanza. Though there a few slightly incongruous, perhaps even a little ominous, words – 'festered', 'rotted', 'heavy', 'punishing' – the general ambience seems to be that of the bright and warm world of childhood innocence. The narrator recounts what appears to be a pleasant, happy memory from childhood; a familiar experience often encouraged by teachers of collecting frogspawn and watching it transform into frogs. How old was Heaney at the time the poem's set? From the simple language Miss Walls uses, such as 'daddy' and 'mammy frog and her delicately worded explanation of frogs mating, we can guess that he was still at primary school or, perhaps, the first years of secondary. So, we might wonder, where/how does death enter this warmly lit, safe-seeming world?

The richness of the flax-dam is conjured by the wealth of sensory images. Visual images – 'green', 'spotted butterflies', 'huge sods'- combine with tactile ones – 'heavy', 'sweltered'. Sometimes Heaney also creates images which appeal to several different senses at the same time. For example, 'bubbles gargled delicately' is visual, tactile and aural, so that we see, hear and can feel the image all at once. At other times, the poet mixes senses more radically, using a device known as 'synaesthesia':

'BluebOtt/es / wOve a strOng gauze Of **sound around** the smell'

In this line sound is converted into a tangible, physical object, a 'gauze' that is 'woven'. The dense sonic texture of the line enhances the mixing effect. As well as the full internal rhyme, other sounds run through the lines, such as the closed and open 'o' and 'u' sounds [ue, ott, ove, au, o, ow] sibilance, alliteration of 'b' and close repetition of 'g'. The metrical pattern is also thickened, with extra stresses: 'ott', 'wove', 'strong', 'gauze', 'sound', 'round', 'smell'. In other words, the line enacts the sense it conveys.

A similar effect is created in the following lines 'the *warm* **thick slob**bER / Of frogspawn that grew like clotted watER'. Heaney bunches stresses together, uses a wonderfully onomatopoeic word, 'slobber', creates internal rhyme with 'slobb' / 'frog' [also echoed in 'of' and 'ott'], and 'warm' / 'spawn'/ 'water'. Plus there's a half-rhyme of 'slobber' and 'water'. To which are added the hard 'c' of 'thick' and 'clott' as well as a run of 'w's in 'warm', 'spawn', 'grew', 'water'. So, this is an unusually sensory, sonically rich and textured style.

Generally in Heaney's poem, rhyme has migrated from the conventional end of lines to crop up internally. Sometimes rhyme is used to manage the rhythm. For instance, 'and wait and **watch** until / the fattening **dots** burst'. Here Heaney's lineation creates a pause at the perfect moment. Another is created through the rhyme of 'dots', which in turn gives the dynamic, dramatic 'burst' greater emphasis by creating a small pause before it. To appreciate the effect, try swapping 'see' for 'watch'. But where, we might still be wondering, is the death mentioned in the title?

The pentameter of the poem's 21$^{st}$ line is broken across the two stanzas. This suggests connection. But the full stop after 'rain' implies separation and difference. Perhaps the 21$^{st}$ line is the fracture point between a before and after. The opening line of this stanza begins 'then one hot day when...' and the poem is back in narrative mode and the reader anticipates that we are moving towards the crux of the story. How much time has elapsed between the two stanzas? Hard to tell, but it seems months or even years, for reasons we'll come back to later. Things are the same - the narrator is visiting the flax-dam - but they are also significantly, world-changingly different.

## The great slime kings

The rich, warm atmosphere has given way now to a much more threatening one. The rot in the first stanza comes to fruition, producing a potent 'rank' smell. The frogs now are 'angry' and, like an aggressive army, they have 'invaded' the flax dam. The noise they make has grown coarser and ominously deeper. The fact that the narrator 'had not heard' these sounds before raises a crucial question:
Had the frogs not made this noise before or had he, somehow, not noticed it before? In other words, is it the flax-dam that has changed or the narrator's perception of it? In the following lines the frogs are described in disgusting, repulsive detail: They are 'gross-bellied', their 'loose necks pulse', their 'blunt heads' are 'farting'. Picking up the military analogy, 'cocked' and 'poised like mud grenades', they are weaponised. And the movement and sounds they make are like 'obscene threats'. A gang of yobbo frogs! Again Heaney employs sonic devices to reinforce his visual images. Take, for example, the

horribly onomatopoeic 'some hopped: / the slap and plop were obscene threats'. In fact, that 'o' sound have previously cropped up in 'cocked' and 'sods' and can be traced back to the source, 'frogs'. With three, swift verbs in half a line, the narrator has scarpered, sure that the frogs had 'gathered' for 'vengeance'. This seems a bit extreme, we might think. Frogs don't feature much in Revenge Tragedies. And yobby froggy revenge for what exactly? And, still, where is this death we were warned about/ promised?

## Fostered alike by beauty and by fear

It seems that the narrator believes the frogs might be about to attack him as revenge for stealing their frogspawn. Correct me if I'm wrong, but it seems a little unlikely that this would really happen. I mean, come off it. So we might conjecture that this vengeance is a figment of the boy/poet's imagination. Or a product of his guilt. Certainly it's hard to imagine the frogspawn would really grow all sci-fi movie monstery, reach out, 'clutch' his hand and presumably drag him into itself to be devoured. [Now that would be a death to justify Heaney's title.] But it's only frogspawn, after all, and grisly murder just isn't going to happen. Heaney quoted the lines above about 'beauty and fear' in his Selected Poems. They are from William Wordsworth's epic of selfhood, The Prelude, an extract from which we consider later in this book. The quote refers to the parental effect nature had in shaping Wordsworth's moral character and poetic sensibility. As important as the beauty of nature in The Prelude is the fear of punishment for transgressions against nature. Heaney's poem can be read in this light; first he is inspired by the wonder of nature; later he is taught a moral lesson about stealing from it. Death of a Naturalist can also be read as a poem about, growing up, about moving from an innocent to an experienced world view. Read in this way, it's not the flax-dam/frogs/nature that's changed, it's the narrator's more grown-up perspective that becomes alert to the danger and darkness in the nature of things.

There's another reading of the poem also connected with the idea of growing up, specifically with moving from being a child to being an adolescent. For delicacy's sake, we won't go into any great detail here, but the reading is triggered by the seemingly disproportionate punishment the narrator fears from the frogs, set up from the start of the poem with the reference to a 'punishing sun'. Add to that Heaney's Catholic upbringing and understanding of sin and guilt, and the references to reproduction. Add to that the references to rottenness and rankness. Add in the transgressive mixing of senses, pervasive sensory overload and the visceral physical disgust at the end. Finally add the descriptions of the 'frogspawn', 'slobber', 'clotted water', 'spawn' with the 'bass chorus'. If you haven't got it yet, you probably never will and we don't suggest you ask a colleague or, worse, a teacher.

Whichever reading you find convincing, an innocent or less innocent one, the collection *Death of a Naturalist* overall is certainly autobiographical, concerned with the shaping of identity, with family relationships and with growing up. An essential part of this growing up is fostered by the poet's interaction with the natural world, by its beauty, but also the fear it could generate in him. But what about that death we kept hearing about, you ask? The death in this poem is, then, of a naive or innocent, childish interaction with the natural world and the consequent birth of a more experienced, less innocent adult perspective. It is a death because, the poem suggests, the loss of childhood innocence felt like a bereavement.

*Death of a Naturalist* crunched:

FESTERED - HEAVY - ROTTED - SWELTERED - GARGLED - GAUZE - SLOBBER - CLOTTED - SPRING - JAMPOTFULS - WATCH - BURST - TADPOLES - DADDY - MAMMY - FROGSPAWN - THEN - ANGRY - INVADED - COARSE - BASS - GROSS - PULSED - OBSCENE - FARTING - SICKENED - VENGEANCE - CLUTCH

# Ted Hughes, *Hawk Roosting*

If you're a teacher, before reading Hughes' poem with a class you could give them just the following lines [if you're a student you might like to have a go at this task, even if you've already read *Hawk Roosting*]:

'I will kill where I please because it is all mine'

'in sleep rehearse perfect kills'

'my eye has permitted no change'

'No arguments assert my right'

'I am going to keep things like this'

'the earth's face upward for my inspection'

'my manners are tearing off heads'

'the allotment of death'

'now I hold Creation in my foot'

Perhaps working in pairs, pupils could discuss what impression they form of the speaker. What are this speaker's key personality traits? As well as what the speaker says, consider too how they say it – how, for instance, would you describe the tone of these lines? Which of the following words are the best fit? Remorseless; savage; honest; murderous; violent; God-like; clear-thinking; psychopathic; arrogant; maniacal; greedy; wise; egotistical; deluded; pitiless;

boastful; obsessive; monstrous; free; cold-blooded; merciless; tyrannical; powerful; individualist; frightening; fascistic; natural.

## Free powers without ethics

The character that emerges from these descriptions is violently murderous and their tone has a matter-of-fact boastfulness that implies a fatal lack of empathy. If they were human they'd be a bloody despot or, perhaps, even a serial killer. And there are definite human aspects of the creature. Hughes could, for example, simply have used the word 'claws', but instead repeatedly refers to the hawk's 'feet' ['hooked feet', 'my foot', 'My feet are locked' etc.] encouraging us to make the human link. As the critic Eric Falci puts it, 'the picture that most often' emerges in Hughes' poems is of 'a violent, atavistic world in which all the substance of civilization and culture is stripped away to reveal primal, base forces that *drive human actions*.'[4] [My italics. 'Atavistic' means reverting to the primitive.]

Of course, in fact, Hughes is trying to imagine himself into the mind of a hawk, but it's a rather human hawk. Some key questions are whether the hawk represents nature as a whole, or whether we should read it, as the bird does, as the pinnacle of creation. Does the hawk represent one violent aspect and perhaps a mouse would represent other gentler aspects of nature. While we may admire Hughes' imagination, we might worry about the ethics, or lack of them. Specifically, what is the poet's attitude to the hawk's character? Is he merely conveying this, or is he either celebrating or condemning it? We don't know, because Hughes does not provide the comforting frame of any narratorial comment. The reader is presented with a troubling picture of nature, bloody in tooth and claw, and must make of it what they will.

After his first two collections, *Hawk in the Rain* [1957] and *Lupercal* [1960] from which *Hawk Roosting* comes, Ted Hughes made his name as a nature poet, or, more specifically an animal poet. Concerned with elemental, natural and mythic forces, his poetry collections are stuffed with poems about animals or poems in the voices of animals. It was one of the ways in which Hughes'

---

[4] Falci, *The Cambridge Introduction to British Poetry 1945-2010*, p.66

poetry was startlingly different from previous, rather sentimental iterations of nature poetry. His subject and style were also entirely opposed to the concerns and aesthetics of The Movement [5] poets who were his contemporaries.

The hawk expressly rejects civilized manners and social and ethical norms, dismissively labelling these as 'falsifying' and as 'sophistry', i.e. sophisticated-sounding falsehood. What we might broadly call 'civilization' or 'culture' would simply get in the way of its instinctual predatory efficiency. Hughes' challenge to the polite, mannered English society of the 1950s is most obvious in the provocatively brutal, 'my manners are tearing off heads'. Tellingly, this phrase suggests the hawk is not simply following its instincts; it takes pleasure, relishes the violence and suffering it inflicts. Nor can civil society simply ignore the hawk, as its single objective, its 'one path', is ominously 'direct' 'through the bones of the living'. Elsewhere, the hawk boldly claims it needs 'no argument' to 'assert' its 'right' to killing. Its behaviour is not a matter of debate, it just, essentially, is, and must always be, like this. It cannot or will not be changed by argument or persuasion; the hawk is absolutely unaffected by societal values or norms or by time: Its behaviour is eternal, 'Nothing has changed since I began'. Moreover, it will fight against any change, 'I am going to keep things like this'. This simple, cold-blooded and blunt language, in typically declarative form, allows no argument or counter view to be expressed.

Perhaps Hughes is implying that when human society becomes too divorced and disconnected from nature it becomes 'unnatural', develops a false understanding of both our own human nature and of the natural world itself. A sentimental attitude to nature and to ourselves shies away from the eternal

---

[5] The Movement's poetry tended to be about social manners, was predominantly urban, urbane and often the tone was rather detached and ironic.

laws of survival. Or we try to apply inappropriate ethical modes of thinking to these natural laws. If we want to relate what Hughes implies about nature to human behaviour perhaps we could place this poem alongside William Golding's 1954 novel *Lord of the Flies* as showing the repressed savagery underneath ordinary social behaviour. Neither Golding nor Hughes are necessarily saying that this savagery is our real, true, 'natural' selves, but rather they remind us we all have the capacity for cruelty and violence, and we should not argue or pretend otherwise. In this sense, Golding's novel and Hughes' early poetry can be seen as a product of, and a response to, the savagery of WWII, a war that featured concentration camps such as Auschwitz and the dropping of atomic bombs on the Japanese city of Hiroshima.

## Nature thinking?

As we've already seen, Hughes' hawk uses some impressively complex vocabulary. As well as 'falsifying' and 'sophistry', the hawk employs superior, polysyllabic words, such as 'convenience', 'buoyancy', 'advantage' and 'inspection'. Indeed, from the opening line its superior character has been established. Not only is it literally at the 'top of the wood', but it also has its 'eyes closed'. This small detail signals that the hawk does not fear anything else in creation and that it is free to ignore everything else and to focus just on its own impulses. It is also, as we have noted, 'above' ethical concerns and manners. Characteristically the bird speaks in a series of blunt statements, the brutality of which is often emphasised by end-stopping. Notice, for instance, how many of the lines in the poem end with full stops. 'I kill where I please because it is all mine,' is a great example. Composed of four curt sentences, each ending with an emphatic full stop, the final stanza is another potent example of this emphatic style.

No metre governs the hawk's free thoughts. Nor is there any principle ordering line length. The longest lines are around ten words long, the shortest has only four words; the longest lines have around five beats, the shortest just two. Such irregularity and roughness of design is the stylistic equivalent of the hawk's rejection of a 'falsifying dream' trying to govern its behaviour. Hughes rejects the falsifying dream of conventional poetic aesthetics - like the hawk - and his poem goes its own way, trusting its own self-generated impulses. Only occasionally does the poem happen upon conventional poetic features, such as rhyme. When it does appear, rhyme functions as a form of demonstrative emphasis, as in 'hooked **feet** / Or in **sleep** rehearse perfect kills and **eat**'. The poem's words are, however, arranged into generally unrhymed, rather irregular quatrains.

With breathless arrogance, the hawk claims the sun is 'behind' it, as if the most powerful natural forces support its stance. Moreover, the bird claims that it 'took the whole of Creation' to produce just its 'foot'. Not only that, it boasts that now it holds Creation in its foot. Perhaps by the capitalisation of creation the hawk implies it is now more powerful than God, the ultimate creator. If we accept this claim, then death has become more powerful than life. For the hawk is a bringer of death and destruction, not a force of creation. Perhaps this is the ultimate hubris and self-delusion of the hawk. Like Satan in John Milton's monumental Christian epic *Paradise Lost*, though it was created by God it now thinks of itself as superior to its creator.

Perhaps this hawk should take note that, for Satan, this turned out to be an extremely foolish and costly bit of sophistry. Perhaps one way of thinking about the form of the poem is that for all the savage freedom the hawk embodies and expresses, it is contained within the frame of both language and the organising, ordering creative will of a superior power to itself, that of its maker, the poet.

*Hawk Roosting* squashed:

TOP - FALSIFYING - FEET - PERFECT - CONVENIENCE - BUOYANCY - ADVANTAGE - INSPECTION - LOCKED - WHOLE - EACH - CREATION - REVOLVE - MINE - SOPHISTRY - MANNERS - DEATH - DIRECT - BONES - RIGHT - BEHIND - CHANGED - PERMITTED - I

# John Keats, *To Autumn*

## Load every rift with ore

In his fascinating poetry primer, *The Secret Life of Poems*, poet and critic Tom Paulin argues that *To Autumn* is a coded political allegory responding to contemporary events such as the Peterloo Massacre and government infringements of liberty. To my mind, Paulin's Marxist reading may be brilliant, but it is also a little tenuous, requiring some tendentious linguistic gymnastics to contort the poem into the interpretation. A couple of examples: Paulin argues Keats's use of the word 'sun' in the first line inevitably conjures a specific loaded rhyme word. Think of a few possibilities for a moment and you might come up with 'run', 'fun', 'pun', 'stun', 'bun', 'spun', 'done'. But Paulin insists that readers automatically arrive at 'gun' which then evokes the violence of the Peterloo Massacre. Similarly, noting the use of the words 'fill, still, and will' Paulin argues that 'ill' 'lurks' within them and this signals unease and even fear of death. The problem is that Paulin wants to make almost every image in the poem fit his political reading and this just seems unconvincing. However, the idea that Keats's poem has a political dimension, that by writing about nature he is also writing about his own liberal ideology is certainly an interesting one and we will return to it later in this essay.

Among other qualities, Keats's poetry is celebrated, and sometimes criticised, for its luxuriant sensory overload. To help appreciate this, try reading the opening stanza with the adjectives and adjectival phrases removed:

'Season of mists and fruitfulness,
Friend of the sun,
Conspiring with him how to load and bless
With fruit the vines that round the eves run.
To bend with apples the trees,
And fill all fruit with ripeness,
To swell the gourd, and plump the hazel shells,
With a kernel; to set budding more
And still more flowers for the bees,
Until they think days will never cease,
For Summer has o'er-brimm'd their cells.'

Without reading the original, try adding a sprinkling of adjectives. If you need a bit of help, here's a list: mellow; close; bosom; maturing; thatch; moss'd; cottage; to the core; sweet; later; warm; clammy. That's more than one adjective per line. That certainly is a liberal sprinkling of adjectives. Of course, the richness isn't generated by the adjectives alone, imagery and Keats's sonic devices are also crucial ingredients.

The imagery in this opening stanza is all about things growing fatter, fuller and riper: The fruit is filled with ripeness; apple trees are so loaded that their branches 'bend'; gourds 'swell', hazels shells are made 'plump', everything is 'budding more/ and still more'; summer hasn't just filled up her stores, they have been filled to spilling, 'oe'r-brimm'd'. Everywhere is plenty, nature's bounty, excess even, fecundity. Keats's imagery also appeals to a wide range of senses. Visual images, such as of the 'maturing sun' and 'vines', mix with tactile ones, such the 'clammy' bees' cells, and with lines that appeal to taste, such as the 'sweet kernel'. And weaving these together Keats's creates an intense musicality in his verse. In the first two lines, for example, sibilance combines with assonance and alliteration:

101

'SeasONs of mist and mellow fruitfulness,
Close bosOM-friend of the maturing sUn.'

The sibilance and long, open 'ee' sound of 'season' are threaded through the whole of the first stanza. Their combined sound runs, for instance, through 'eves' to 'trees' and on to 'sweet' and 'bees' to 'cease' and appears prominently in three end rhymes.

## Like a gleaner

Addressing 'her' directly, in the second stanza Keats personifies autumn as a sort of pagan goddess. For a goddess, she's found, however, not in heavenly palaces but in very ordinary agricultural places, such as 'a granary floor'. For a goddess, she's also not remote in any way and she doesn't appear to have favourites or a priesthood - 'whoever seeks abroad may find' her. She's also a very chilled seeming goddess, as presumably 'careless' means without cares. Further evidence for her untroubled tranquility is that she can be found 'fast asleep', intoxicated by 'the fume of poppies'. Evidently she's also not terribly industrious, leaving off her tasks to have a good old midday nap. Hence the 'furrow' remains only 'half-reap'd' and her 'hook' has spared the 'next swath' of  flowers. Oddly, she sometimes likes to lie like a human/goddess bridge across a stream, or perhaps rather this image suggests she crosses a brook steadilty. She also likes to watch cider being made, presumably in anticipation of trying a glass or two of the fruity nectar. As in the first stanza, Keats weaves a sonically intense texture, especially in the last line. Compare for instance, 'you watch the last oozings by the hour', which has the same overt sense, but none of the rich, syrupy music.

Tom Paulin's comments on the personification of autumn are helpful and interesting. Paulin argues that the use of a 'gleaner' rather than another synonym for a farm-hand or agricultural labourer is politically significant

102

because a gleaner was 'a member of the rural poor...who has scraped up the grains of corn left after the farm labourers had gathered in the harvest.' Moreover, 'gleaning was made illegal in 1818, so by personifying autumn as a gleaner he is characterising the season as a proud and dignified young woman'. Keats's goddess is a rather humble, agricultural one and, as the first stanza showed, she is generous and her bounty is life-sustaining. Hence, by making a gleaner a goddess, the poet is showing his respect, solidarity with, and veneration for the working poor.

Keats was a second generation Romantic poet. Like many of the Romantics, his radical aesthetic principles were aligned with his political radicalism. In particular, Keats held politically liberal sympathies and had liberal friends, such as the poet and publisher, Leigh Hunt. Like Hunt, Keats criticised monarchy and protested against social injustice. Like Hunt, he was subject to politically motivated excoriating reviews. Unlike Hunt, Keats was, however, never imprisoned for his radicalism. By celebrating nature over culture, Keats reveals a political as well as aesthetic orientation. He rejects the urban and the sophisticated and the wealthy and the upper classes; his appreciation of beauty is centred squarely on what is free to all of us, the natural world. His embodiment of this beauty is an ordinary peasant woman whose work had been criminalised.

## Easeful death

Many critics have noted the change in tone in the final stanza of *To Autumn*. Broadly speaking the first stanza presented the positive aspects of late summer, the second focuses on autumn as a goddess and the last moves into more elegiac mood. Light, for instance, is leaving the landscape, so that the day is 'soft-dying'. The wind, a traditional symbol of animation and imagination grows inconstant, it 'lives or dies'. A choir of gnats are said to 'mourn / among the river sallows'. The final image, of swallows, gathering in the sky suggests departure and draws on classical poetic convention: Traditionally birds taking off and flying away is a symbol of death.

As darkness begins to fall, the last stanza of Keats's ode is dominated by sonic imagery, the music of autumn. As well as the choir of gnats, lambs 'bleat', crickets 'sing', a robin 'whistles' and the swallows 'twitter'. These noises are not clamorous or discordant; there doesn't seem to be any great resistance to, or unhappiness about, the onward march of time and the consequent intimations of mortality. Like the gnats, it seems the poet is content to be 'borne aloft' or to 'sink' by the 'light wind' of fate. This tranquil mood of acceptance recalls lines from Keats's *Ode to a Nightingale*: '...for many a time / I have been half in love with easeful death'. As with the sensory sensuality of Keats's poems, some critics have objected to this sentiment, arguing that it is unhealthy or unmanly or decadent.

What they fail to acknowledge is the active will and force of imagination of the poet who orchestrates this material into beautifully composed verse; an act of creative, shaping and artistic will to set against the poem's more overt

 sentiments. And was it really surprising that a medically trained poet, one who had nursed his younger brother through his fatal consumption and who knew when he himself coughed up blood that it was arterial blood and therefore his own death sentence, that he was most in love with beauty that is the verge of being lost? For Keats, beauty was made even more beautiful by being transient, at its most radiant in the moments before it gave in to decay. He is intoxicated by the final 'bloom' and 'rosy hue' of the 'soft-dying day' on the 'stubble-plains' [surely an image suggesting the last moments of life leaving a human face]. This was not some decadent aesthetic affectation, but the real lived experience of a poet who was dead by the age of just 25.

***To Autumn*** distilled:

**FRUITFULNESS - SUN - BLESS - VINES - APPLES - RIPENESS - PLUMP -
BUDDING - FLOWERS - NEVER - OE'R-BRIMMED - OFT - WHOEVER -
GRANARY - SOFT-LIFTED - ASLEEP - DROWS'D - SPARES - GLEANER -
BROOK - PATIENT - OOZINGS - SONGS - MUSIC - SOFT-DYING - ROSY -
WAILFUL - BORNE - WIND - BLEAT - SING - WHISTLES - SWALLOWS**

# Philip Larkin, *Afternoons*

## At the edge of a crowd

Despite expressing some unpalatable views on a range of issues, most controversially on race, class and gender, Philip Larkin was indisputably a great poet, certainly one of the foremost English poets of the second half of the twentieth century. Erudite and a critical success, Larkin was that rare beast, a poet who was also popular with a general readership who actually bought his books. The bookish, jazz-loving, unmarried, cycling academic librarian developed a gloomy Eeyorish public persona and many of his poems are infected with a profound bleakness. Famous examples include *This Be the Verse* which begins with an obscenity suggesting parents have a damaging effect on their children and ends with the magnificently bleak: 'Man passes on misery to man/ It deepens like a coastal shelf/ Get out as early as you can/ and don't have any kids yourself'! But in his best poems, tenderness and beauty counterbalance the temperamental depressiveness, and they are so hard won that they seem even more beautiful and precious and true. The same poet who wrote *This Be the Verse* also produced the final line, 'what survives of us is love' [though, characteristically, Larkin hedged this idealistic sentiment by saying it might prove 'almost true'].

The foremost member of The Movement poets, Larkin had a sharp, often satirical eye and as often a sardonic tongue. Like other Movement poets, his writing is characterised by the skillful use of traditional English forms, by an ironic outsider stance, by its candour and by the poet's deployment of a mix of slangy modern idiom with more elevated 'poetic' diction. Often it sounds in his poems as if the poet is simply speaking to us in his memorably pithy voice. It's a highly distinctive voice, 'plain-speaking, sceptical, modest, unshowy, awkward, common-sensical'.[6]

*Afternoons* demonstrates both the off-putting and positive qualities of Larkin's verse. We might be put-off by the whiff of snobbishness in the way the poet observes the working-class subjects of the poem. The men, for instance, are a collective, not individuals, as if they are indistinguishable from each other and defined by their work. There's  something of the social anthropologist about Larkin's persona in this poem, and he seems to view these working-class people from a housing estate almost as if there were from an alien culture. On the other hand, he expresses empathy towards the young mothers. Larkin does not merely observe them as if through a lense, he feels for them, shares and understands their feelings of a lack of control and agency in their lives: 'something is pushing them/ to the sides of their own lives'.

## Photographs, not a film

*Afternoons* typifies Larkin's poems. It starts on the cusp of a season we might associate with the poet, almost autumn. The temporal setting is late summer, a time when the brightest season is losing its vigour, warmth and energy; it is 'fading'. Leaves are beginning to fall from the trees. The language is down-to-earth, unshowy and conversational, the style understated. There are no

---

[6] Hamilton & Noel-Todd, *Oxford Companion to Modern Poetry*, pp.325-338

ostentatious metaphors or startlingly original combinations of diction. The second line, for instance, is comprised of six very ordinary monosyllables. The physical setting of a 'recreation ground' is also an ordinary one. And in this ordinary setting, the people are doing ordinary, commonplace things; the children are playing while the adults stand around and watch. The scene is, however, curiously orderly, energyless, almost, in fact, static: Even the leaves fall in 'ones and twos' and the men 'stand', as if statues, 'at intervals'. The opening is composed like a series of photographs, rather than a film. The whole thing is very visual, but the sound channel has been entirely muted. The atmosphere is almost sterile, almost oppressive: women 'assemble', as if ordered to do so; the men 'stand' apart in their separate stanza. The children have been 'set free' as if, normally they are prisoners. There also doesn't seem to be any communication or connection between the women, the men, the children or between each group. For a description of a playground there's a distinct lack of excitement, movement or, indeed, play. The poem's form also contributes to this pervasive sense of enervation. Larkin employs three eight line stanzas, or octets, so that the same pattern is repeated three times.

The general sense of down-beat, low-keyness is also evident from what the poem lacks. Check it for musical qualities and you'll find precious few. There's no metre, so no pulse or beat to keep the lines ticking over. Nor is there any rhyme, apart from a bit of seemingly incidental assonance between 'two' and 'noons'. Search for other sonic effects, such as alliteration or onomatopoeia and you'll return empty-handed. Larkin's language is not only not inflated, it's actively flat or deflated. Even the few figurative phrases are understated: 'the hollows of afternoons' may synaesthetically turn time into an object, but it's not a particularly original idea and there's no semantic complexity for the reader to wrestle with.

We quickly get the idea of an empty period. There's also a bit of effective hyperbole; 'an estateful of washing' neatly conveys the sheer scale of the drudgery in these women's lives. Similarly, the reference to the wedding album 'lying/ near to the television' implies that romance has been side-lined and perhaps that it always was a misrepresentation of reality, a lie of sorts. Perhaps too there's some symbolism in the 'wind' that is ruining the courting-places, as in the wind of time. 'Beauty thickened' also makes an abstract idea concrete, but, as with the 'hollow' metaphor it's easily understood; basically, as the women have got older, they've also grown fatter. We might also read those short adverbial phrases, 'behind them' and 'before them' symbolically, with the women stuck or trapped between the two. There are several ways in which the men might be considered 'behind' the women [such as being a part of their past] and the wind 'before them' suggests that the image of ruination is a projection of their future.

## No airy consolations

Overall Larkin presents a characteristically bleak picture of the emptiness of modern life. He's sometimes seen as the pre-eminent Post-war poet and his take on society certainly seems shadowed by WWII and the austerity that followed. The picture is warmed a little, though, by the empathy the poet feels for the women. We might guess too that the general idea he pulls from this specific scene, that 'something' we cannot quite name or recognise sets the direction of our lives, that we are not really in control of how our lives turn out, might apply as much to Larkin as to the women and, indeed, to all of us. As the critic Michael Schmidt comments, Larkin is 'a poet who speaks bleak truths' and he is therefore 'probably more valuable than one who gives us airy and empty consolations'.[7] If you're after airy consolations, look elsewhere.

*Afternoons* crunched:


FADING – FALL – BORDERING – NEW – HOLLOWS – MOTHERS –
SWING – CHILDREN – INTERVALS – STAND – ESTATEFUL – ALBUMS –
LYING – TELEVISION – BEFORE – RUINING – STILL – SCHOOL –
CHILDREN – ACORNS – HOME – THICKENED - SOMETHING – SIDE

---

[7] Schmidt, *Lives of the Poets*, p.811

# Wilfred Owen, *Dulce et Decorum est*

The verbs associated with the narrator begin with the first person plural pronoun 'we': 'we cursed;' 'we turned'; 'we trudge'. Immediately the reader understands that the poem is describing a collective, group experience. In these conditions the soldiers are not differentiated by rank [officer or private] or by class [upper, middle or lower]; they are all in a horrific situation together, respond in the same way and suffer equally. And the poet is also part of this experience. The focus shifts from the group to intense personal and individual experience when Owen employs the first person singular in the line *'As under a green sea I saw him drowning'*. The active verb changes to the passive in the lines that follow, signalling mutual helplessness:

'He plunges at **me**'

The change to the personal pronouns emphasises Owen's dual role, as both a participant and witness to these events. He was performing a similar role to modern journalists, embedded with the army, reporting on battles. Unlike journalists, however, Owen does not observe from the outside; he was a captain in the English army and he is fully engaged in the action. In the last shift of focus Owen tries to build a virtual bridge spanning from the trenches of WWI to the comfort of home, and for modern readers of this visceral war poem, from the distant past to the present day. Across this space Owen asks us to imagine witnessing the horrors he witnessed: 'If **you** could hear...the blood/ come gargling from the froth-corrupted lungs'.

## Smothering dreams

Like many other soldiers of the First World War, Owen suffered terribly from shell shock. Indeed, he was invalided to Craiglockhart Hospital in Scotland, and it was here that he was encouraged to turn his traumatic war time experiences into poems. Officers generally suffered more from mental illness, nervous breakdowns, hysteria and so forth, than their men. This may have been because they were responsible for looking after soldiers in a situation where this was virtually impossible to do, in situations where death could come suddenly without warning, seemingly at random.

The symptoms of shell shock varied from man to man: Owen's friend Siegfried Sassoon suffered hallucinations, other soldiers went mute or developed hypersensitivity to loud sounds. Wilfred Owen's shell shock manifested itself in vivid nightmares:

'In all my dreams, before my helpless sight'
He plunges at me, guttering, choking, drowning'.

After this anguished personal line, Owen pulls back into the collective experience, 'the wagon that **we** flung him in'.

In the last stanza of the poet seems almost to lift his head out of the poem and speak directly to his 'friend'. And to us. The simple, but powerful device of the second person pronoun, 'you' connects us to Owen's experience and makes us reflect on our attitudes to war and to war propaganda in all its forms.

111

Owen's description of the dying soldier suggests he felt a sense of responsibility and that, perhaps, this is the reason why he is haunted by the man's death in 'all' his dreams. Notice how Owen uses the present continuous participle of *'smothering'* as an adjective to describe the dreams. Grammatically this links Owen with the dying soldier. The poet also experiences feelings of suffocation in his dreams, just as the man had in life. Owen's feelings of sadness and guilt harden in the last stanza and convert to anger. Anger projected at people back home who had no understanding of the atrocious conditions on the front lines. In particular Owen rages against propagandists who present war as a great adventure, as 'sweet and glorious'. His poem is a powerful corrective to such romanticized ideas

of war. See, for example, Tennyson's *The Charge of the Light Brigade* or Rupert Brooke's idealistic *The Soldier*.

## Anti-propaganda

Think of an image you would use for recruiting to the British Army. What would you choose? An image of brave, strong, happy, handsome and youthful men in smart uniforms doing exciting, manly work in exotic locations, perhaps? Look again at the images of the soldiers in the first stanza of *Dulce et Decorum Est*. Four things stand out about how they are presented:

1. They have been crippled by the weight of their suffering. They are 'bent double', and 'knock-kneed', so disabled they can hardly walk, or see or hear; they are 'lame', 'blind' and 'deaf'.

2. Owen uses two shocking similes:

- The soldiers are 'like old **beggars**'
- They are 'coughing like **hags**'.

The comparison to 'beggars' expresses their desperate and shabby state. The simple adjective 'old' shows how the trauma of battle has prematurely aged and enfeebled the men. 'Hags' refers to witch-like, ugly old women, so in this image the men are aged and emasculated. This means their strength and masculinity has been drained away.

3. Their morale is shot to pieces. They are exhausted: The soldiers 'curse' and 'trudge' and are 'drunk with fatigue'. In other words, they are so tired they are almost senseless, oblivious to the dangers around them.

4. In any situation their state would be awful and pitiable. How much worse though to be so desperately vulnerable so close to the front lines? When they most need to be alert to save their lives, the soldiers responses are numbed. Out of their minds, they turn 'their backs' on flares; 'blind' and 'deaf' to the sounds of shells ('five-nines') falling behind them they stumble onwards.

The overall impression is of men on their very last legs, almost zombified, almost the walking dead. If they were to meet German troops now they would be annihilated. The phrase *'distant rest'* metaphorically implies death. Owen implies that these half-dead men are trudging slowly towards inevitable death. The insistent plosive and fricative alliterations - 'bent' and 'beggars'; 'knock-kneed'; 'coughing' and 'cursed', supported by the assonance of 'sacks' and 'hags', 'knock' and 'cough', generate the ponderousness and heaviness of the poem's opening stanza.

## Someone was yelling out

As we have seen, the poem starts with the group, but then zooms in to focus on the death of one man. Enhanced by Owen's sudden switch to the present tense, the urgent direct speech makes the scene tense and immediate: 'Gas! Gas! Quick boys!' After the gas explodes the soldier has only moments to fit the respirator that would save his life. In the chaos  and confusion he is too slow. The next moment he is 'yelling and stumbling'. The dynamic verb 'plunges' conveys desperation, implying simultaneously the uncontrolled violence of his movement, the idea of water and of sudden depths.

The physical agony suffered by this man is conveyed through the simile of being on fire. Three present continuous participles [look at the all the words in these two stanzas ending with '-ing'] takes us into the scene, as if it is happening before us. And the moment is held frozen for three horrible beats, 'guttering, choking, drowning'. In the final stanza, further gruesome, hard-hitting images, both visual, such as his eyes 'writhing' and aural/tactile - 'the blood come gargling' - convey the grotesque suffering of the soldier.

## My Friends

Owen addresses his audience ironically as 'my friend'. The tone he is sardonic, darkly ironic. Originally Owen addressed this poem to a particular person, Jessie Pope, a poet who had written many recruiting poems, including the famous *Who's for the game*? In the title Pope uses a popular euphemism for war, comparing it to sport.  Owen is enraged by how writers misrepresented the reality of war, particularly those, like Pope who had no direct experience of battle. Hence he is saying if 'you' could have witnessed this horror you would not encourage children to think of war as 'sweet and glorious'. The choice of the quotation from the Latin poet Horace suggests that writers throughout history have romanticised the experience of war, and Owen's poem is a repudiation of easy and trite patriotic sentiments. The broken nature of the quotation suggests the brokenness of its sentiment. The

114

'high zest' he refers to is the enthusiastic relish of war propagandists, and how it infects boys, who become 'desperate' and 'ardent' for such 'glory'.

Beyond Pope, Horace and other writers, Owen is addressing all the people back home. Many soldiers felt anger at the ignorance of those in England, particularly at the warmongers, those people keenest for the war to continue. Famously Sassoon issued a declaration, published in The Times newspaper, in which he called for the end of what he considered to have become a war of aggression, not liberation:

I believe that I may help to destroy the callous complacency with which the majority of those at home regard the contrivance of agonies which they do not, and which they have not sufficient imagination to realize.

Some of the soldiers who fought in the First World War were just seventeen years old. Most of the millions killed on both sides were young men. Owen, himself, died in his mid-twenties. Those who signed up had little or no idea of the reality of modern trench warfare. They had told of the adventure of a lifetime, as the most glorious of sports; they found blasted landscapes, rats and lice, the rain and mud, no man's land and barbed wire, endless artillery bombardment and gas attacks, bits of bodies of the dead in the trench walls, mechanised death on a monumental scale. Owen felt deeply the essential innocence of the soldiers. The children in the poem represent this and the next, impressionable and easily exploited generation, 'ardent for some desperate glory' of the heroic sort depicted in this painting.

## Wilfred Owen's photographs

Imagine the poem as a series of frames with specific camera angles and it will help you to understand the poet's intensely visual, filmic technique.

- The first stanza is like a long, slow, sweeping, wide angled shot, showing the whole troop or brigade.
- After the sudden exclamatory shout of 'Gas! Gas!' the camera angles cut much more quickly.
- The camera spins to find the 'someone' who is the dying man.
- In the tense moment that follows it is as if the screen goes blank; we know something awful has happened, but we cannot see what it is; we are left only with disembodied sound of 'yelling out'.
- When we do see the man 'floundering' our perspective is initially objective; we are watching him from close by.
- Next the description switches to what is called a point-of-view shot, where the audience looks through the eyes of a character. For one claustrophobic moment we are inside the gas mask looking through Owen's eyes:

'Dim through the misty pains and thick green light
as under a green sea, I saw him drowning.'

Picking up the verb 'plunges', the scale of the visual simile of a 'green sea' implies the extraordinary speed with which the gas spreads and the soldier is engulfed and dying. A later simile implies that the soldiers are in hell, the man's face, 'is like a devil's sick of sin'.

Again Owen switches between different types of sensory imagery. The idea of sin and sickness are carried forward in the sonically explosive simile, 'obscene as cancer' and in 'vile incurable sores'. Tactile and taste imagery create a sense of intimate experience, 'bitter...on tongues', further forcing the reader to imagine the experience and recoil in horror from it.

## Breaking down

Owen's poem is written in **iambic pentameter**, a metre often used in English for poems with serious themes. The lines fall into a roughly iambic pattern, but this metre is often bent, warped and overloaded, as if by the stress of the content. Look, for example, at the first two lines:

'Bent, double, like old beggars under sacks'
'Knock-kneed, coughing like hags we cursed through sludge'

'Bent', 'old' and 'kneed' could and probably should be stressed. Hence the first two beats of the first two lines of the poem contain extra stresses and are weightier and slower than a regular iambic pattern. The technical term for the double stresses ['bent, doub' and 'knock-kneed'] is a spondee. Elsewhere the iambic metre is so put under such strain that it verges on breaking down. Look, for instance, at lines such as:

'Gas! Gas! Quick boys! – an ecstasy of fumbling'
'and watch the white eyes writhing in his face'.

The first of these lines starts with a double spondee, creating extra stress. It's like the rapid volley of stresses, like gunfire: TUM TUM TUM TUM. Even if we added an unstressed beat for the emphatic caesura, you can see that the iambic pattern is breaking down.

The central tension in the poem is between order and fragmentation, control and degeneration. The title, for example, is the incomplete, broken off first half of a quotation. Many of the lines in the poem are broken down by caesuras; consequently, the rhythm is often faltering. Extra stresses, as in the first two lines, and the intense emotional charge create the impression of a poem almost breaking out of its formal constraints. There is order here, but it is under immense stress. Mirroring the half quotation title, for instance, the final stanza ends with a fragmentary half line, 'pro patria mori'.

Tension is also conveyed through the ordering pattern of rhyme, working against the irregular, uneven pattern of stanzas:

- the first stanza is 8 lines
- the second has 6 lines
- the third only 2
- and the final stanza has 12.

Similarly, the two-line stanza effectively isolates, but also connects the dying man to Owen: The dying man lives on only in the poet's dreams. Put all those lines together and the poem is twenty-eight lines long, a double sonnet, surely bitterly ironic form considering the subject matter.

Owen set himself the challenging task of writing a poem that is meant to sound like natural impassioned speech within the constraints of a regular iambic metre and a regular cross-rhyme pattern (ABAB CDCD etc.) At times he very skilfully uses enjambment and caesura for mimetic effect. By 'mimetic' we mean that *the way* he says something conveys the experience just as much as *what* he is saying.

Look once again at the first two lines:

'Bent-double, like old beggars under sacks,
Knock-kneed, coughing like hags, we cursed through sludge.'

He could just have easily have written, 'we cursed through sludge, bent like old beggars, knock-kneed and coughing like hags'. Is there any difference?

Yes, Owen's opening is static; the sentence's subject (the men) and verbal action (cursed) are held back by the syntax. Four consecutive adjectival clauses result in the reader being left uncertain about who or what is being described. The effect is to make the verse seems to stagger along – look at how those commas create a halting, arrested movement, mimetic of that of the soldiers' weary tread.

## Owen's war

A young man joining up to fight would have no idea at all what the reality of fighting would have been like. The First World War was the first fully mechanised war, with mustard gas, machine guns and tanks. The nature of trench warfare was profoundly different to battle in previous wars, being essentially attritional. The numbers speak for themselves:

- Eight million soldiers were killed
- Including civilians about twenty million people died
- On just the first day of the battle of the Somme, twenty thousand men were killed, sixty thousand injured. That's one man dead or injured every second for twenty-four hours.
- Life expectancy of a junior officer: 1 month.

Wilfred Owen wrote a number of contradictory things about war and poetry. In his preface to his collection of war poems, for instance, he said he was 'above all...not concerned with Poetry', but that "The Poetry is in the Pity'. By this he was seeking to make a distinction between self-consciously stylised and elevated grand Poetry and the poetry he was writing, which was more grounded in reality, more concerned with truth than style.

Owen also called himself a 'conscientious objector with a very seared conscience'. In other words, he felt deeply ambivalent about the war and his role in it. There was a powerful tension in his character between different conceptions of himself. On the one side was the Christian, poetic self - sensitive, compassionate and romantic, in love with the works of Romantic poets, such as Keats and Shelley. On the other side was the soldierly self; disciplined, manly, ordered, heroic, stoical. Much of Owen's best poet springs from this internal conflict.

*Dulce et Decorum Est* is an angry poem, a poem in which the poet tries desperately hard to make readers imagine the horror, the pity and the waste of life he witnessed. But, it's wrong to see it as simply an anti-war poem, though often it has been read as such. The real target of Owen's fury is war propaganda. Look at how that last stanza, comprising one long sentence, builds and builds momentum, as horrific detail is piled on horrific detail with words are almost spat out until it reaches its climactic blunt and direct repudiation of 'the old lie'.

**Dulce et Decorum Est** crunched:

**BEGGARS – HAGS - HAUNTING – REST- ASLEEP – BLIND – DEAF - FIVE-NINES – GAS – CLUMSY – SOMEONE – FIRE – GREEN – SEA – DREAMS – DROWNING – SMOTHERING – FLUNG – WRITHING – SIN – BLOOD – OBSCENE – INCURABLE – FRIEND – CHILDREN – LIE – MORI**

# Percy Bysshe Shelley, *Ozymandias*

## Man vs. nature & time

In a sense, Shelley's poem has three narrators:

1. the author of the inscription
2. the first-person voice
3. and words by or put in the mouth of the subject of the sculpture, Ozymandias aka the Egyptian Pharaoh Ramasses II.

The little piece of recorded speech is related by the traveller, and hence enclosed within the traveller's narration. And all that the traveller says is related to us by the first speaker, the poet, and so enclosed by the poet. This device of several enclosed narratives, rather like a Russian doll, means that Shelley can delineate the desert and the Pharaoh, their vastness and power, but at the same time control and enclose them as miniatures inside his field of powerful language, his poem.

The traveller from 'an antique land' provides an exotic element to the poem and an implied contrast with the poet's more limited experience. Romantic poets, such as Blake, Wordsworth and Shelley were drawn to solitary individuals who quested after knowledge, wisdom and understanding. This quest often took them to some sort of sublime natural environment, such as a mountain range or a desert. It is characteristic of the Romantics to find wisdom far away from civilisation and the comforts of home.

The Pharaoh, Ramasses, is an emblem of autocratic political power: 'the sneer of cold command'. He is presented as hubristic, i.e. so full of his own self-importance that he is due a fall. Arrogance and vanity are demonstrated by his having a statue erected to himself on which he has the extraordinarily vain and foolish words, 'king of kings' engraved. However magnificent and indomitable Ramesses thought himself, Shelley shows, however, how puny

his power was against the vast might of nature and of time. So, Shelley's poem warns tyrants that however impregnable their position may appear to be, they are, in reality, vulnerable. To less powerful, ordinary people this is a message of political hope.

The unnamed and unknown artist is a kindred spirit for the poet. Part of the poem's business is to assert and demonstrate the primacy and permanence of forms created by art over the more transient trappings of worldly power. Time, however, has changed the meaning of the statue, with the vainglorious inscription now resonating ironically against the blank emptiness of the desert.

The imagery gives the reader a sense of the exotic through the traveller, the antique land, and the extraordinary name, 'Ozymandias'. Shelley also includes images of desolation and destruction, such as the trunkless legs, shattered visage, decay, desert, sand and the wreck. Violence is also suggested generally through the wreckage, as well as specific verbs, such as 'shattered' and 'stamped'.

The scale of the statue is conveyed through the adjectives, 'vast' and 'colossal'. Yet this huge wreckage is dwarfed by the enormity of nature, here in its perhaps most desolate form, the desert. The adjectival phrase 'boundless and bare' implies the desert is both endless and endlessly featureless, a sense of an eternity of nothingness enhanced in the final line, 'the lone and level sands stretch away'. There is a suggestion here of the desert as time and the endless time of death.

## Sounds in the desert

The sound 'and' occurs fifteen times. That's a lot for a fourteen-line poem, and that repetition of sound, coupled with its sense of going on, of continuing, adding, helps give the poem its drive and momentum. Also the rhyme scheme, abab acdc edef ef holds the poem tightly together, giving the reader an impression of something unified and complete. Notice how the first rhyme 'land' is passed from the first four-line stanza, or quatrain, to the second, 'command', the seventh rhyme, 'things' runs into the third quatrain, and the eighth, 'appear' continues into the final couplet. Internal rhyme of 'Round' and 'boundless' with the assonance of 'nothing', 'colossal' and 'lone' set up the finish by helping to slow and steady the reader. This change of tempo is reinforced by sonic qualities:

- the alliteration of 'boundless and bare' and 'lone and level'
- and the dominant drawn out long 'o' and 'ow' sounds.

One interesting syntactical device Shelley employs in this poem is the use of two adjectives connected by 'and': 'vast and trunkless', 'boundless and bare', 'lone and level'. These give the reader a sense of full and yet qualified description, a double vision of the object described. It's an economical technique that helps give us the impression of a real landscape the poet is capturing rather than creating.

*Ozymandias* is a sonnet, although as we saw above the rhyme scheme isn't traditional. There is no obvious break in the pattern where you might expect the volta, or 'turn'. The 'turn' is change in direction in a poem, a feature of traditional sonnets where, usually after the octave, there is a change or shift in emphasis or argument, or a new subject or angle is introduced. And indeed, there is no turn in this sonnet. One thing that makes this poem so innovative is the way that instead of a neat argument, with a turn after line eight and a flourish at the end, as per a conventional sonnet, the structure here is one of enclosure: Three statements creating three little worlds within them. This delivers a tremendously powerful sense of unity, and allows the poet and the reader to play with and control scale in a seemingly effortless way.

Shelley is an expert at speeding up and slowing the reader down, so that the rhythm of the words underscores the meaning. The following two examples illustrate this point nicely:

- The line 'look on my words, ye Mighty, and despair' has only four stresses and so trips along quickly: TUM ti – ti TUM   ti-TUM, ti-  ti TUM
- This creates a contrast with the following half line which is much slower, 'Nothing beside remains', TUM-ti ti-TUM ti-TUM.

Even though almost all of this poem is reported speech, and natural enough sounding, it still fits the sonnet form, without seeming in any way forced. That shows considerable skill. And though the lines would sound wrong read as iambic pentameter, that rhythm is there as part of the poem's sonic substratum, its deep undersong.

Enjambment is the running of sentences over the line breaks; caesura is the splitting of lines with a pause. These two devices work together to run against the regular pattern of the rhyme scheme. They help to convey the sense of a speaking voice, making the words sound more natural by reducing the emphasis at the end of each line. Look at the end-stopped lines: They come at the end of the octave:

- line 8, '…and the heart that fed'
- line 11, '…and despair'
- and in the final level with its unequivocal full stop.

The effect is to lend greater emphasis to these particular rhyme words. The poem runs up in a long sentence to '<u>fed</u>', a word that conveys how much the ordinary people relied on the 'heart', signifying emotions of the Pharaoh. Shelley wanted to emphasise 'despair' and 'away' for obvious reasons. The caesuras in the final lines are particularly effective. The pauses after 'nothing beside remains' and 'colossal wreck' allow the absoluteness of the phrases to sink in, as well as suggesting momentarily empty or emptied space.

## Stretching far away…

Friend of Lord Byron and John Keats, husband of the writer of *Frankenstein*, Mary Shelley, Percy Bysshe Shelley was part of the second generation of Romantic poets which had followed the trail blazed by Blake, Wordsworth and Coleridge. A political idealist, like Blake, Shelley expressed strongly anti-establishment views. Indeed, Shelley's views were so radical and incendiary that little of his work was published in his lifetime. Like Blake, Shelley was writing at a time of great political volatility in the turbulent years that followed the French Revolution.

In *Ozymandias* Shelley asserts the enduring power of art and artists over that of kings, pharaohs and in particular tyrants. Like other Romantics, Shelley also shows how the creations of man are made to seem minute when set against nature and the cosmic dimension of time. Nevertheless, unlike the statue it depicts, Shelley's poem looks set to endure.

**Ozymandias** crunched:

Obviously, this process will always be a personal one. This is just one possibility. Do it yourself and see where we agree and disagree. What have you spotted that we have not?

**ANTIQUE – TRUNKLESS – DESERT – VISAGE – SNEER – SCULPTOR – LIFELESS – MOCKED – PEDESTAL – OZYMANDIAS – DESPAIR – DECAY – WRECK – SANDS**

(One sign of this poem's greatness is the fact that it could be 'crunched' in many interesting ways – every single word tells.)

# Owen Sheers, *Mametz Wood*

## Chits of bone

Like the painting above by Christopher Williams, Sheers' moving, poignant poem commemorates a bloody attack by the Welsh Fusiliers on a fortified

German position in Mametz wood, one of the many sub-battles of the infamous Battle of the Somme [1916]. The poem seems perfectly suited for a cloze exercise, as this will draw attention to some of the poet's more striking language choices. If you're a teacher, you could present the poem to a class with the following words blanked out: 'wasted young'; 'chit'; 'china plate'; 'relic'; 'bird's egg'; 'nesting'; 'sentinel'; 'wound'; 'foreign body'; 'skin'; 'broken mosaic'; 'socketed'; 'dropped open'; 'notes'; 'sung' and 'absent tongues'. If you're a student, consider what each of this list of words contributes to the poem.

The first phrase, 'wasted young', recalls Wilfred Owen's references to 'doomed youth' and to the soldiers as 'boys'. They are 'wasted' in two senses, both wasted away, decayed, but also, more feelingly, their deaths were a waste. The phrase keeps in mind the fact that some of the soldiers would have been only teenagers when they fought and died in the trenches of WWI.

The next four words and phrases work together to establish the fragility of the remains and the tenderness with which the poem handles them. A 'chit' is a small piece of paper; hence the metaphor suggests the bones have become very delicate and thin. A 'chit' is often issued for something owed, which raises the idea of what we might owe these men. It can also mean a small child or baby animal. The 'china plate' metaphor enhances the impression, conjuring a visual image of broken crockery. With its religious connotations, 'relic' may take us in a slightly different direction, but also confirms the poet's attitude of veneration for the dead. The last image in this series is the most powerful. Comparing the skull to a 'bird's egg' is visually haunting and conveys the horrible vulnerability of flesh and blood to violence. The overall effect of  the second stanza is enhanced by Sheers' use of sonic devices. In the first line, emphatic metre picks out the important words:

'A **chit** of **b**one, the **chi**na **plate** of a **sh**oulder **b**lade'

Alliteration of 'ch' modulates into the softer 'sh' and 'bone' alliterates with 'blade'; assonantal rhyme connects 'plate' to 'blade' and 'china plate' near rhymes with 'shoulder blade'. The 'pl' and 'bl' sounds are echoed in the next line, combining with the full rhyme of '<u>b</u>one', giving '<u>b</u>lown' greater emphasis. These plosive and assonantal sounds climax in '<u>b</u>roken <u>b</u>ird'.

Similarly, Sheers uses imagery and sound for emphasis in the reference to the machine guns in the next stanza. Metaphorically they are 'nesting', an image that recalls the 'bird's egg' and might make us think of cuckoos or other birds which steal other birds' nests. The terrible factual detail that soldiers in the Somme were ordered to 'walk, not run' into gunfire is powerful enough by itself, but in a poem in which end rhyme is used only here, the couplet it forms with 'guns' is especially effective and affecting.

## Even now the earth stands sentinel

'Sentinel' obviously makes us think of military guards or look-outs. Personifying the 'earth' in this way creates a counterbalance to the idea that the soldiers' lives were 'wasted'. It is as if nature now guards them because they are precious and her own. Though nothing can be done to help these dead men, the poem suggests that, like 'the earth' what we can do is honour and remember them. Personification continues in the image of the earth as a wounded victim of war working out a 'foreign body'. Like the simple references to time, 'for years', 'even now', it reminds  us how long lasting, how deep the devastation of the war was and how widespread; a hundred years on and the land is still recovering, and still uncovering more dead.

The broken dead. Like Armitage in *The Manhunt*, Sheers has already presented the men's body as fragments, bits of body parts - bone, skull, shoulder-blades. And these fragments are themselves 'broken'. Found buried together, the bodies are a 'broken mosaic' and the skulls of some are missing jaws. In a horrible irony, their worthless boots have 'outlasted them'. And yet the men seem almost alive - their skeletons have been 'paused mid dance macabre', as if the poet or time could press a button and set them moving again in a morbid dance of life-in-death. The image of their 'socketed' heads is another morbid one, but set against this brokenness and morbidity is the men's emphatic togetherness. They are a 'they'; one 'mosaic'; 'their' heads and 'their skeletons', and, most poignantly, even in death they are 'linked arm in arm'.

The men obviously cannot sing or indeed tell their story. But this 'unearthing' - the revelation of their graves - prompts another unearthing of their story, this poem, the words Sheers has used, the reading of it in every reader's mind. In this way, Sheers, like the earth, stands sentinel over these men's grave and offers his voice to speak for their 'absent tongues'.

Why, you might ask, has Sheers written the poem in tercets - three-lined stanzas? Good question and the truth is, I don't know. There is, however, something delicate about tercets in comparison to more robust quatrains. And Sheers adds to this delicacy through using quite long lines stretched out across the page. Maybe he was thinking too of the three central relationships in the poem - the soldiers, nature and us. Like the poet, we did not experience the horrors these young men suffered. All we can do is to continue to honour and remember their sacrifice, and stand like sentinels to their memories for the sake of future generations.

*Mametz Wood* crunched:

AFTERWARDS - WASTED - TENDED - BONE - FINGER - SKULL - MIMICKED - WALK - GUNS - SENTINEL - BACK - WOUND - GRAVE - MOSAIC - SKELETONS - OUTLASTED - HEADS - OPEN - SUNG - UNEARTHING - ABSENT

# William Wordsworth, *Excerpt from The Prelude*

## Epic of the self

This extract comes from the first section of a much longer poem, *The Prelude or, Growth of a Poet's Mind*, [1850] on which Wordsworth worked for most of his adult life and which ran to fourteen 'chapters' and almost eight thousand lines! Wordsworth had set out to write an epic poem to rival John Milton's monumental masterpiece, *Paradise Lost*. Epic poems are long narrative poems that explore historical or mythological events important to the culture in which they are written. Milton's poem traced the fall of Adam and Eve from the Garden of Eden into a world of sin and death; Wordsworth, in a turn of Romantic individualism, cast himself as the hero of his own epic and wrote *The Prelude* to examine the significant moments from his own life that had led him to becoming a poet and which had shaped his understanding of the world. However, like Milton, Wordsworth chose to compose his poem in blank verse, unrhymed lines of five stressed syllables usually with an iambic metre. This not only enabled Wordsworth to replicate the natural rhythms of everyday speech - a particular concern of the Romantic poets - but also gave him the flexibility to relate and unfold events for the reader in the naturalistic and organic way he actually experienced them, rather than distort experience by forcing it to conform to a strict rhyme scheme or inflexible metrical pattern.

As its subtitle, 'Childhood and school time', indicates in this first section Wordsworth dramatises key episodes in his early life growing up in the Lake District, tracing the ways in which his moral consciousness and poetic sensibility were shaped by his interactions with the natural world. His close friend, and fellow Romantic poet, Coleridge called nature, the 'Great Universal Teacher' and repeatedly Wordsworth presents experiences in which nature takes on an instructive or parental role. 'Fostered' alike by nature's 'beauty and fear', the poet describes himself as shaped by nature's 'ministry'. Characteristically, episodes from the opening section of *The Prelude* feature a vivid memory of childhood experience followed by an explanation of how nature impressed a particular lesson onto the young poet's heart and mind. Just before this excerpt, for example, Wordsworth recounts the theft of a boat which he rowed across a dark lake. He's not got far across the lake before he is admonished for this act of stealth by a huge, dark craggy ridge that seems to rise up before him and loom ominously over him.

## The loud pack chiming

In comparison, this extract seems untroubled, the focus more on the joy of being young, carefree and among friends. Swiftly Wordsworth paints the scene for us. It is a cold and crisp, a 'frosty' season and a time between day and night, 'twilight'. In the almost darkness the cottage windows 'blazed' with light and warmth. The boy is free to follow his own playful impulses; he pays no attention to the 'summons' to return home. He is not merely 'happy' like his friends, Wordsworth rejoices and revels in his liberty; 'for me / it was a time of rapture'. Happy memory indeed! As the simile comparing himself to a horse evinces, he feels a part of nature, full of unbridled energy and boundless potential. Simultaneously the poet/ boy is alone in his thoughts, an 'I' but also part of a group of children, a 'we' playing exuberant games of chase, lost in the physical pleasure of vigorous exercise.

The episode is animated by a combination of visual and aural imagery: We see the blazing cottage light in the gloom; we hear the village clock, 'clear and loud'; we see the boy as he 'wheeled about', hear the 'resounding horn'; see the stars 'sparkling clear', hear how the ice 'tinkled'. At times the poet uses sonic devices, such as sibilance and assonance to mimic the sounds of action. Probably the clearest example of this onomatopoeic effect is the description of skating:

'All shod with steel / we hissed along the polished ice in games'

The sonic skimming effect is generated here by the co-ordination of sibilance with the soft 'sh' sounds, the assonance of short 'o's and a run of liquidy 'l's.

The blissful, busy harmoniousness of the scene is emphasised by the unusual and unlikely verb Wordsworth uses to describe the clamour of a pack of hounds: 'The loud pack chiming'. Chiming, of course, carries two senses, both which are resonant in this scene - the melodious ringing of bells and being in accord with someone or something. Not only do the dogs 'chime' with the children's pleasure, the whole landscape echoes and amplifies their joy: 'with the din / smitten, the precipices rang aloud'. 'Every icy crag' joins in, so that there seems to be universal rapture. Like 'chiming', the verb 'smitten' catches the eye, and the ear. Wordsworth gives the word a little sonic push forward into our consciousness through the near rhyme with 'din' [near in both proximity and sound], by placing 'smitten' prominently at the start of the line and by reversing the metrical foot. Scan back up the page and you'll see all the previous lines have begun with a regular iambic pattern, unstress/ stress, except for '**proud** and exulting'. Since that excpetion, seven iambic openings to lines have followed in a row. So,  naturally we hit the trochee, '**smitt**en', a bit harder than we otherwise would have done. And, of course, the verb also personifies the landscape, as if it has been brought alive by the children. Not only that, but 'smitten' is associated with suddenly falling in love, with delirious happiness.

Wordsworth believed that men of special poetic genius had a more refined sensibility and more acute sensitivity than ordinary folk. Even as a boy he seems more attuned to the soul of the universe than his 'confederates', because in this seemingly unsullied, innocent and joyous scene, Wordsworth's powerful poetic antennae picks up from 'far distant hills' a different music, 'an alien sound'. Only briefly does this different tone of 'melancholy' impinge on his happy thoughts; it has, he says, not gone 'unnoticed'. But this is enough to change the atmosphere of the closing lines of this excerpt. What sadness can there be in such a happy scene? Perhaps only the awareness that it cannot last, that night must come. Perhaps the sparkling stars are like the children and the 'orange sky of evening' is time inevitably passing. That would explain the use of the final phrase 'died away'. It is the consciousness of mortality, perhaps, that sets the poet apart. Such an intervention, or lesson, at the end of an episode is entirely characteristic of the pattern of *The Prelude* as a whole.

## Working in harmony

As we have seen, the vibrancy of this extract is generated by the rich visual and aural imagery and the preponderance of bright, musical words, such as 'blazed', 'tolled', 'chiming', 'rang', 'tinkled', 'hissed', 'din' and 'sparkling'. To this list can be added words that reveal Wordsworth's heightened feelings, 'rapture', 'exulting', 'happy', 'tumult'. Along with verbs like 'flew' and 'blazed', the last word in that list is also part of a series that create the sense of energy. But the imagery and the words don't do all the work; the sentence construction, syntax, metre and punctuation also play a major part in generating the verse's dynamism.

The opening lines start with the simplest conjunction 'and', immediately conveying the fact that this is another example in a series that illustrate a central idea. This sentence runs for six enjambed lines to arrive at its exclamatory conclusion 'rapture!' The last sentence of the extract is longer still: From 'so through darkness' it sweeps over nine mostly enjambed lines. Whenever you find as much enjambment in a poem as this, you know that the language is almost running away with itself, like the boy as a horse wheeling about, it is almost escaping control. That fact that Wordsworth has chosen blank verse, i.e. unrhymed pentameter aids the flow, as the ear is not stopped even momentarily by rhyme sounds at the ends of lines. The metre does its part too. Maintaining control, it also keeps the verse ticking nicely along. Wordsworth's iambic pentameter is almost as regular as clockwork. Take, for example, the first line: 'And **in** the **frosty seas**on **when** the **sun'** or these two:

'It **was** in**deed** for **all** of **us** - for **me**
It **was** a **time** of **rapt**ure! **Clear** and **loud'**

Only a few hard-pressed full stops arrest the poem's irresistible onward momentum. Only three hold back the tide of words in the whole extract. As common are those most uncertain and zippiest of punctuation marks, dashes. Linking phrases or clauses together, dashes aid rather than arrest the flow. Semi-colons are used the most of any punctuation. Five semi-colons indicate Wordsworth's tendency to write in lists. The overall effect is of language skimming along, like those skates over the polished ice.

***Excerpt from The Prelude*** crunched:

**FROSTY - BLAZED - SUMMONS - US - RAPTURE - TOLLED - HORSE - STEEL - ICE - CONFEDERATE - PLEASURES - CHIMING - DARKNESS - DIN - SMITTEN - EVERY - TINKLED - ALIEN - MELANCHOLY - SPARKLING - AWAY**

Such a wonderful description of a cherished childhood memory could be the

catalyst for some creative writing. What are some of your own happiest childhood memories? Why not re-live one of these by writing about it? It doesn't have to be for anyone other than yourself. We cannot turn back time, of course, but with endless capacities of language and the power of our imaginations we can get pretty darn close to time travel.

'Poetry is everywhere; it just needs editing.'

JAMES TATE

# A sonnet of revision activities

1.  Reverse millionaire: 10,000 points if students can guess the poem just from one word from it. You can vary the difficulty as much as you like. For example, 'clams', would be fairly easily identifiable as from Sexton's poem whereas 'fleet' would be more difficult. 1000 points if students can name the poem from a single phrase or image – 'portion out the stars and dates'. 100 points for a single line. 10 points for recognising the poem from a stanza. Play individually or in teams.

2.  Research the poet. Find one sentence about them that you think sheds light on their poem in the anthology. Compare with your classmates. Or find a couple more lines or a stanza by a poet and see if others can recognise the writer from their lines.

3.  Write a cento based on one or more of the poems. A cento is a poem constructed from lines from other poems. Difficult, creative, but also fun, perhaps.

4.  Read 3 or 4 other poems by one of the poets. Write a pastiche. See if classmates can recognise the poet you're imitating.

5.  Write the introduction for a critical guide on the poems aimed at next year's yr. 10 class.

6.  Use the poet Glynn Maxwell's typology of poems to arrange the poems into different groups. In his excellent book, *On Poetry*, Maxwell suggests poems have four dominant aspects, which he calls solar, lunar, musical and visual. A solar poem hits home, is immediately striking. A lunar poem, by contrast, is more mysterious and might not give up its meanings so easily. Ideally a lunar poem will haunt your imagination. Written mainly for the ear, a musical poem focuses on the sounds of language, rather than the meanings. Think of Lewis Carroll's

*Jabberwocky.* A visual poem is self-conscious about how it looks to the eye. Concrete poems are the ultimate visual poems. According to Maxwell, the very best poems are strong in each dimension. Try applying this test to each poem. Which ones come out on top?

7. Maxwell also recommends conceptualising the context in which the words of the poem are created or spoken. Which poems would suit being read around a camp fire? Which would be better declaimed from the top of a tall building? Which might you imagine on a stage? Which ones are more like conversation overheard? Which are the easiest and which the most difficult to place?

8. Mr Maxwell is a fund of interesting ideas. He suggests all poems dramatise a battle between the forces of whiteness and blackness, nothingness and somethingness, sound and silence, life and death. In each poem, what is the dynamic between whiteness and blackness? Which appears to have the upper hand?

9. Still thinking in terms of evaluation, consider the winnowing effect of time. Which of the modern poems do you think might be still read in 20, a 100 or 200 years? Why?

10. Give yourself only the first and last line of one of the poems. Without peeking at the original, try to fill in the middle. Easy level: write in prose. Expert level: attempt verse.

11. According to Russian Formalist critics, poetry performs a 'controlled explosion on ordinary language'. What evidence can you find in this selection of controlled linguistic detonations?

12. A famous musician once said that though he wasn't the best at playing all the notes, nobody played the silences better. In Japanese garden water features the sound of a water drop is designed to make us notice the silence around it. Try reading one of the poems in the light of these

comments, focusing on the use of white space, caesuras, punctuation – all the devices that create the silence on which the noise of the poem rests.

13. In *Notes on the Art of Poetry*, Dylan Thomas wrote that 'the best craftsmanship always leaves holes and gaps in the works of the poem so that something that is not in the poem can creep, crawl, flash or thunder in'. Examine a poem in the light of this comment, looking for its holes and gaps. If you discover these, what 'creeps', 'crawls' or 'flashes' in to fill them?

14. Different types of poems conceive the purpose of poetry differently. Broadly speaking Augustan poets of the eighteenth century aimed to impress their readers with the wit of their ideas and the elegance of the expression. In contrast, Romantic poets wished to move their readers' hearts. Characteristically Victorian poets aimed to teach the readers some kind of moral principle or example. Self-involved, avant-garde Modernists weren't overly bothered about finding, never mind pleasing, a general audience. What impact do the Eduqas anthology poems seek? Do they seek to amuse, appeal to the heart, teach us something? Are they like soliloquies – the overheard inner workings of thinking – or more like speeches or mini-plays? Try placing each poem somewhere on the following continuums. Then create a few continuums of your own. As ever, comparison with your classmates will prove illuminating.

Emotional.............................................................................intellectual

Feelings........................................................................................ideas

Internal...................................................................................external

Contemplative....................................................................rhetorical

Open..........................................................................................guarded

# Terminology task

The following is a list of poetry terminology and short definitions of the terms. Unfortunately, cruel, malicious individuals [i.e. us] have scrambled them up. Your task is to unscramble the list, matching each term to the correct definition. Good luck!

| Term | Definition |
|---|---|
| Imagery | Vowel rhyme, e.g. 'bat' and 'lag' |
| Metre | An implicit comparison in which one thing is said to be another |
| Rhythm | |
| Simile | Description in poetry |
| Metaphor | A conventional metaphor, such as a 'dove' for peace |
| Symbol | A metrical foot comprising an unstressed followed by a stressed beat |
| Iambic | |
| Pentameter | A line with five beats |
| Enjambment | Description in poetry using metaphor, simile or personification |
| Caesura | |
| Dramatic monologue | A repeated pattern of ordered sound |
| Figurative imagery | An explicit comparison of two things, using 'like' or 'as' |
| Onomatopoeia | Words, or combinations of words, whose sounds mimic their meaning |
| Lyric | |
| Adjective | Words in a line starting with the same letter or sound |
| Alliteration | A strong break in a line, usually signalled by punctuation |
| Ballad | A regular pattern of beats in each line |
| Sonnet | A narrative poem with an alternating four and three beat line |
| Assonance | |
| Sensory imagery | A word that describes a noun |
| Quatrain | A 14-line poem following several possible rhyme schemes |
| Diction | When a sentence steps over the end of a line and continues into the next line or stanza |
| Personification | |
| | Description that uses the senses |
| | A four-line stanza |
| | Inanimate objects given human characteristics |
| | A poem written in the voice of a character |
| | A poem written in the first person, focusing on the emotional experience of the narrator |
| | A term to describe the vocabulary used in a poem. |

# GLOSSARY

ALLITERATION – the repetition of consonants at the start of neighbouring words in a line

ANAPAEST - a three beat pattern of syllables, unstress, unstress, stress. E.g. 'on the moon', 'to the coast', 'anapaest'

ANTITHESIS - the use of balanced opposites

APOSTROPHE – a figure of speech addressing a person, object or idea

ASSONANCE – vowel rhyme, e.g. sod and block

BLANK VERSE – unrhymed lines of iambic pentameter

BLAZON – a male lover describing the parts of his beloved

CADENCE – the rise of fall of sounds in a line of poetry

CAESURA – a distinct break in a poetic line, usually marked by punctuation

COMPLAINT – a type of love poem concerned with loss and mourning

CONCEIT – an extended metaphor

CONSONANCE – rhyme based on consonants only, e.g. book and back

COUPLET – a two-line stanza, conventionally rhyming

DACTYL – the reverse pattern to the anapaest; stress, unstress, unstress. E.g. 'Strong as a'

DRAMATIC MONOLOGUE – a poem written in the voice of a distinct character

ELEGY – a poem in mourning for someone dead

END-RHYME – rhyming words at the end of a line

END-STOPPED – the opposite of enjambment; i.e. when the sentence and the poetic line stop at the same point

ENJAMBMENT – where sentences run over the end of lines and stanzas

FIGURATIVE LANGUAGE – language that is not literal, but employs figures of speech, such as metaphor, simile and personification

FEMININE RHYME – a rhyme that ends with an unstressed syllable or unstressed syllables.

FREE VERSE – poetry without metre or a regular, set form

GOTHIC – a style of literature characterised by psychological horror, dark deeds and uncanny events

HEROIC COUPLETS – pairs of rhymed lines in iambic pentameter

HYPERBOLE – extreme exaggeration

IAMBIC – a metrical pattern of a weak followed by a strong stress, ti-TUM, like a heart beat

IMAGERY – the umbrella term for description in poetry. Sensory imagery refers to descriptions that appeal to sight, sound and so forth; figurative imagery refers to the use of devices such as metaphor, simile and personification

JUXTAPOSITION – two things placed together to create a strong contrast

LYRIC – an emotional, personal poem usually with a first-person speaker

MASCULINE RHYME – an end rhyme on a strong syllable

METAPHOR – an implicit comparison in which one thing is said to be another

METAPHYSICAL – a type of poetry characterised by wit and extended metaphors

METRE – the regular pattern organising sound and rhythm in a poem

MOTIF – a repeated image or pattern of language, often carrying thematic significance

OCTET OR OCTAVE – the opening eight lines of a sonnet

ONOMATOPOEIA – bang, crash, wallop

PENTAMETER – a poetic line consisting of five beats

PERSONIFICATION – giving human characteristics to inanimate things

PLOSIVE – a type of alliteration using 'p' and 'b' sounds

QUATRAIN – a four-line stanza

REFRAIN – a line or lines repeated like a chorus

ROMANTIC – A type of poetry characterised by a love of nature, by strong emotion and heightened tone

SESTET – the last six lines in a sonnet

SIMILE – an explicit comparison of two different things

SONNET – a form of poetry with fourteen lines and a variety of possible set rhyme patterns

SPONDEE – two strong stresses together in a line of poetry

STANZA – the technical name for a verse

SYMBOL – something that stands in for something else. Often a concrete representation of an idea.

SYNTAX – the word order in a sentence. doesn't Without sense English syntax make. Syntax is crucial to sense: For example, though it uses all the same words, 'the man eats the fish' is not the same as 'the fish eats the man'

TERCET – a three-line stanza

TETRAMETER – a line of poetry consisting of four beats

TROCHEE – the opposite of an iamb; stress, unstress, strong, weak.

VILLANELLE – a complex interlocking verse form in which lines are recycled

VOLTA – the 'turn' in a sonnet from the octave to the sestet

# Recommended reading

Atherton, C. & Green, A. Teaching English Literature 16-19. NATE, 2013

Bate, J. Ted Hughes, The Unauthorised Life. William Collins, 2016

Bowen et al. The Art of Poetry, vol.1-4. Peripeteia Press, 2015-16

Brinton, I. Contemporary Poetry. CUP, 2009

Eagleton, T. How to Read a Poem. Wiley & Sons, 2006

Fry, S. The Ode Less Travelled. Arrow, 2007

Hamilton, I. & Noel-Todd, J. Oxford Companion to Modern Poetry, OUP, 2014

Heaney, S. The Government of the Tongue. Farrar, Straus & Giroux, 1976

Herbert, W. & Hollis, M. Strong Words. Bloodaxe, 2000

Howarth, P. The Cambridge Introduction to Modernist Poetry. CUP, 2012

Hurley, M. & O'Neill, M. Poetic Form, An Introduction. CUP, 2012

Meally, M. & Bowen, N. The Art of Writing English Literature Essays, Peripeteia Press, 2014

Maxwell, G. On Poetry. Oberon Masters, 2012

Padel, R. 52 Ways of Looking at a Poem. Vintage, 2004

Padel, R. The Poem and the Journey. Vintage, 2008

Paulin, T. The Secret Life of Poems. Faber & Faber, 2011

Schmidt, M. Lives of the Poets, Orion, 1998

Wolosky, S. The Art of Poetry: How to Read a Poem. OUP, 2008.

# About the author

Head of English and freelance writer, Neil Bowen has a Masters Degree in Literature & Education from Cambridge University and is a member of Ofqual's experts panel for English. He is the author of *The Art of Writing English Essays for GCSE*, co-author of *The Art of Writing English Essays for A-level and Beyond* and of *The Art of Poetry*, volumes 1-10. Neil runs the peripeteia project, bridging the gap between A-level and degree level English courses: www.peripeteia.webs.com.

## Valentine #2

Not a spray of roses or box of chocs.
I give you a pair of my old pants.
Though they are only one
They are also a pair.
(Like us).

Here, have them.

They might blind you with tears –
Like boxers,
Only they're actually y-fronts –
(Cotton, Marks & Sparks)

Not a hotel in Paris or candlelit dinner.
I give you my old pants.
You look like you're crying.

Take them. Please.
They've holes in some inconvenient places.
I am trying to tell the truth.

Though their elastic's gone,
If you pull them apart
Hard enough
The will ping back together.

A bit like us,
hopefully.

**One pound per copy of this book will go to the Ballanta Music Academy in Sierra Leone and to other educational projects in that county.**